THE
StorySeller
Adventures

Kristy,

Thank you for
your support - I
appreciate you!

Erica Michaels

THE
StorySeller
Adventures

A Modern
Allegory
and
Step-By-Step
Guide

How to Grow an Epic Business
and Find More Meaning in Your Work

GIBRAN NICHOLAS

HOUNDSTOOTH
PRESS

THE STORYSELLER ADVENTURES

How to Grow an Epic Business and Find More Meaning in Your Work

ISBN   978-1-5445-3876-1   *Hardcover*

         978-1-5445-3877-8   *Paperback*

         978-1-5445-3878-5   *Ebook*

         978-1-5445-3831-0   *Audiobook*

Contents

To Mandy, the love of my life, and to our children,
Valentina, Marcos, and Marcelo.

Introduction

Dear Reader,

This book is written for people like us, who want to *do work that matters, make a meaningful difference,* and *grow our business.* We're looking for new, practical ideas that we can apply right away to our day-to-day work. We're also looking for spiritual inspiration of some sort because our work connects with us on a deep personal and spiritual level.

To find both, we can draw on the wisdom of the ancient philosophers, wisdom that is surprisingly accessible to us in our world today, and in the context of our business, if only we know where to look.

That's why I have written this book—to take the thousands of years of human experience, the trials and tribulations of those who came before us, and the great teachings of all the great religions and distill them into a simple message, a message that makes sense to modern-day leaders, sales professionals, and entrepreneurs like us.

If any of this describes you and what you're looking for, I think you and your team will enjoy this book! If not, this may not be the right book for you. It's not for everybody, and that's okay.

What's StorySelling?

My goal in writing this book is to help you and your team use StorySelling to stay motivated and grow your business. *Story-Selling is about using the language, structure, and characters of a story to sell more effectively—to sell the best version of yourself to yourself and to sell the best version of your ideal clients to your ideal clients.*

A good story needs three elements: a hero, a villain, and some conflict. The best StorySellers accurately identify the heroes and villains in their own lives and in their clients' lives. Then they create solutions to beat those villains and win the conflict.

That's what we're focused on in this book. We're going to use story elements and characters to better understand ourselves, the people around us, and our experiences. The result is that you and each member of your team will be able to use Story-Selling to

- build your personal brand and improve your sales and marketing results,

- stand out from your competition and articulate your unique value in today's supercompetitive market,

- overcome roadblocks in your personal and professional relationships, and improve your communication results, and

- gain the clarity and confidence you need to launch the next chapter of your life and business.

To accomplish all of this, we need a new way of looking at sales and a new vocabulary for doing so. Let's start with the basics.

What's an Allegory?

This book is an allegory, which is a story written like a novel with valuable lessons that we can apply to our life or business. My favorite allegories have a bit of magical realism (like *The Alchemist*), some fantasy (like *The Arabian Nights*), some business lessons (like *The Greatest Salesman in the World*), and some spiritual themes (like *The Prophet*).

Personally, I love those types of allegories! But I understand not everyone does. That's why Part II contains a "plain language" step-by-step guide for how to use StorySelling and each of the nine human archetypes explored in the story.

If you don't like allegories with magical realism, fantasy, business lessons, and spiritual themes, feel free to skip ahead to Part II. Don't worry—I won't be offended! Either way, you'll walk away with a proven system to grow your business.

What's an Archetype?

The characters, places, and "Realms of Reality" we encounter in this story are called archetypes. An archetype can refer to a personality type, persona, or perspective with common themes or elements. For example, consider American politics at the time of this writing. A certain set of characteristics pop into your mind when I say someone is a Republican or a Democrat. You automatically assume certain things about that person based on the archetype of the political label they wear. If you want to communicate effectively with either a Republican or a Democrat, you'll need to appeal to what's important to them based on their archetype, their persona, their perspective.

In life and business, I've found that people exhibit certain characteristics based on their archetype, which I define as their frame of mind at the moment I encounter them. It's not that they're always that way in all circumstances. It's simply that they're that way now, based on what's important to them at this particular time in their life or business.

For example, a Warrior is someone who is entrenched in a battle, in pursuit of victory. That's their reality at the moment. The best way to earn their business is to give them the tools they need to win their battle and achieve their victory. An Explorer, on the other hand, is "just looking" and may be more interested in the experience of getting somewhere or shopping for something. A Ruler is most often interested in bottom-line results, and so on.

The thing is, though, that people don't wear a label on their forehead that says, "I'm archetype X or Y. Sell to me or communicate with me in this way if you want to earn my business right now." Or maybe they do if we look closely enough. That's what we're doing in this book. We're looking more closely at the nine most common human archetypes, and we're exploring these archetypes in story format.

But Wait, There's More!

In Part II of this book, you'll get a step-by-step guide and coaching tips for each archetype:

- **Your Story:** How to use each archetype to build your personal brand and improve your marketing results.

- **Your Client's Story:** How to use each archetype to overcome client objections.

- **Your Market's Story:** How to use each archetype to stand out from your competition.

- **Your Sales Process:** How to use each archetype to save time and be more productive.

- **Your Business Strategy:** How to use each archetype to trigger profitable shifts in your business strategy.

This approach will help you recognize patterns in your own life and business, as well as in the types of people you encounter. Once you recognize these patterns, you'll be better equipped to earn their business or otherwise win their support. You'll also be able to better understand your own experiences in the context of your own story. That's why the lessons in this book will help you *find more meaning in your work* AND *grow your business*.

What's My Background?

While this book is written in allegory format, it contains real-life stories and lessons I've learned from my experiences and throughout my travels as an entrepreneur and modern-day salesman.

I started my journey as an entrepreneur at a very young age. When I was fifteen, I took an exam called College-Level Examination Program (CLEP). This gave me college credit without having to go to college and allowed me to enter law school at that age, which I did. My goal was to eventually become the youngest-ever president of the United States and change the world. If there was ever a young idealist who had potential, drive, and passion, it was me. But life happened, and I dropped out of law school a year later.

When I was sixteen, I started working in my family's business, helping them to build it from the ground up. Then I started my own business at twenty. I became a millionaire by twenty-five and lost everything by the time I turned twenty-seven. I spent the next decade rebuilding my life and business, learning many lessons along the way. I share with you many of those lessons in this book.

When I turned forty, though, something inside of me rebelled against the life I was living at that time. I was a successful businessman, married to a gorgeous wife, living with our three beautiful children. But I wasn't happy. I wondered how I went from wanting to change the world at sixteen to being just content enough to get through another day at forty. I was burned out, and I needed a total reset.

In the middle of my burnout, I began to look at my life as an allegory and at the characters, including myself, as archetypes. My life's story and my business journeys finally started making a little sense to me! In fact, I got the reset I badly needed by looking at my life and business through the lens of the nine archetypes explored in this book.

It was a life-changing experience, and I made many life-changing decisions as a result. I refocused on the things in my life and career that mattered most to me as a human being: things like being more present when with my family and creating more "white space" in my calendar. This freed up time for me to think, exercise, read, and study.

I was able to get to the root cause of what was really stressing me out and preventing my personal and professional growth. Then I created systems to eliminate and/or "tame the chaos." I exited one business and completely restructured another. I forged new relationships and let go of others. I went in a new direction, and I experienced better results. Today, just two years later, I'm reinvigorated and reenergized, and I'm experiencing breakthroughs in life and business I never imagined possible.

One of the decisions I made through that experience was to write this book! In fact, *The StorySeller Adventures* is the first of a three-book series. It also comes with a coaching program called *The StorySeller 30-Day Business Growth Journey*. You can enroll for free at TheStorySeller.com. This entire book series, along with *The StorySeller 30-Day Business Growth Journey*, is designed to help you avoid some of the mistakes I made that led to my midlife burnout. It's also designed to help those of you who may be experiencing something similar to what I have experienced.

If you read this book and take *The StorySeller 30-Day Business Growth Journey* with me, you'll be able to use Story-Selling and the nine human archetypes to achieve victory in twelve key areas of your life and business. You will learn the following:

1. How to find your Unique, Authentic Winning Story (UAWS): This is the absolute best possible version of yourself and how you sell *that* version of yourself to your ideal client. It's the unique, authentic value you bring to your personal and professional relationships. It's the magic formula that makes you uniquely you, and your story uniquely attractive. Once you find your UAWS, you'll be able to:

    a. find more meaning in your work,

    b. identify your target market and your ideal client,

    c. beat new competitors who have crazy budgets, and

    d. beat entrenched competitors who already own the market.

2. How to simplify and restructure your workload so you have more fun, face less stress, and experience more joy in your day-to-day work.

3. How to identify the specific causes of burnout in your life and business, and how to create boundaries and systems to "tame the chaos."

4. How to stay profitable when profit margins are shrinking and costs are rising.

5. How to use the current economic uncertainty and changing market to your advantage.

6. How to grow your business without spending enormous amounts of money.

7. How to supercharge your strategic relationships to get better results in less time.

8. How to create sustainable growth and momentum in your life and business even when "life happens."

9. How to overcome resistance, corporate politics, family politics, and other roadblocks you encounter when you try to do your work or live your life.

10. How to stop coworkers from sabotaging your efforts, and how to realign the conflicting or unreasonable expectations of clients and strategic partners.

11. How to stay accountable, not lose interest, and get more consistent results in life and business.

12. How to answer these two questions you may be facing in your life and business:

    a. What's next?

    b. What's it all for?

BONUS FOR TEAM LEADERS: How to help your team do all the above!

As of the time of this writing, I've had the privilege and honor of training and coaching over ten thousand sales and business professionals, mostly in the housing and financial industry. In my twenty-plus years of business experience, I've found that the best way for my clients and me to learn is through story.

My goal in sharing my true story in allegory format, along with the step-by-step guide to the nine archetypes and *The Story-Seller 30-Day Business Growth Journey,* is to help you and your team immediately apply the lessons and themes to your day-to-day work and business.

I've found that allegories and archetypes speak to me wherever I am in my journey, and I hope this book speaks to you wherever you are in your journey.

Enjoy!
—Gibran

The Voice
That Called Me

"We decided to go in another direction. I'm sure you understand."

But I didn't understand. So I asked, "Which direction is that?"

"We decided to work with your competitor."

"My competitor?"

"Yeah."

"Which one?"

"The premium one."

"The premium one?"

"Yeah...we really liked their story."

"What story?"

"Well, we just feel like they're a better fit. I'm sure you understand."

Here we go again…I don't ****ing understand! That's what I'm trying to tell you, idiot.

This conversation was going nowhere. So I thanked the would-be clients for their time and ended it.

These people should be thanking me for my time, and here I am saying please and thank you like a damned fool.

I had literally spent months following up with these people, and many days of my life walking them through their options. I had sacrificed family time, personal time, and all sorts of other time to help them. Then, in an instant, they expected me to understand what I simply could not understand.

It wasn't losing the sale that bothered me. It was the ridiculous way in which these particular clients expected me to "understand."

I felt as though I deserved better than this…that my kids deserved better than this. It seemed as if my future, *their* future, was being written in a language I didn't understand, by strangers I didn't identify with, in an industry I didn't recognize anymore.

Just then, as I was wallowing in maximum self-pity, my phone rang. So I answered it.

"Hello?"

"Yes, hello. Is this The StorySeller?"

"What?"

"Are you The StorySeller?"

"Um...I think you have the wrong number."

"No, wait. I was told that you could help me."

"Help you what?"

"Help me find my Story."

"Well, like I said, I think you have the wrong number."

"No, wait. You *are* The StorySeller, aren't you?"

"Dude. You have the wrong number, and I'm hanging up now."

"No, please. I need...I need...I need you to help me find my Story."

"Look. I'm not sure who gave you my phone number, but I'm not a storyteller. I'm a salesman. Please take me off your list."

"Aren't you the one who just lost a sale?"

"Wait...what?" Now I was starting to get annoyed. *How did this stranger know I just lost a sale?* But the Voice repeated the question.

"Aren't you the one who just lost a sale earlier today? Hello?"

"I'm here."

"Well?"

"Well, what?"

"Well, are you going to help me find my Story?"

"Look. I don't know how you found out I lost a sale, and I certainly don't know why you think it has anything to do with you or finding your Story. Are you pranking me?"

"No. But if you could help me find my Story, I guarantee you'll never lose another sale again."

Now I could be certain this was a weird joke. So I decided to play along, just for kicks and giggles.

"So, you're telling me that if I help you find your 'Story'—whatever that means—you can guarantee me that I'll never lose a sale again?"

"Yes."

"That's impossible."

"No, it's not."

"Yes, it is."

"There's only one way for you to find out."

"What's that?"

"The only way for you to see if I'm lying is to stop your self-denying. Help me find my Story. You've really got to try. Or wonder what would have happened until the day you die."

"Hmm. You got me there!"

"I'm not trying to get you here or there; I'm not trying to get you anywhere. I just need you to help me find my Story."

"What makes you so sure that I can help you?"

"Well, you are The StorySeller, aren't you?"

"I told you. I'm...I'm a salesman. I'm not a storyteller."

"All salesmen, all saleswomen, all salespersons are storytellers. Some tell false stories disguised as truth, and others tell true stories that come in all sorts of disguises. The truly great salespeople of the modern age get a call like this, from someone like me, and they answer it. So now that you've answered my call, the next step is for you to help me find my Story. In the words of your modern generation, 'Help me discover and live my truth.' Do you think you can do that for me?"

"Who are you?"

"I'm the future version of you."

"What?!"

I was starting to get confused. I tried to think. *What was I drinking before I got this weird phone call?*

"Hello? Are you there?"

"Look. I'm still here, but I don't think this is real life. I'm hanging up now." Then I went to bed.

The next day, I woke up and thought about that strange phone call. In fact, I thought about it for weeks, and months, and years, until it became a distant memory—a memory belonging to the person I once was...a person full of hope and excitement for the future. And now? I was just a burned-out forty-year-old salesman.

My father was a great salesman, and his father before him was also a great salesman. As for me, I just wasn't sure of my place in this world. It's a big world, but a small one too. It's big enough that you can get lost and small enough that you can get lost in front of everyone you know. It's quite embarrassing actually, getting lost. It's certainly not fun; I can tell you that much. Have you ever felt lost before?

I'm chuckling as I write this. Here I am, talking to myself, about myself, all by myself. But wait, there's more!

I hear my phone ring in the background. I'm gonna answer it.

"Hello?"

"Yes, hello. Is this The StorySeller?"

"What?"

"Are you The StorySeller?"

I sit up straight in my chair. *Here we go again. I could hear the Voice on the other end of the line, but I was struggling to understand what it wanted from me.*

"I'm afraid this is your last chance, pal."

"My last chance for what?"

"This is your last chance to help me find my Story...*your* Story. You need to find your Story before it's too late. Your competitors are nipping at your heels. Your clients are abandoning you. You're in grave danger of becoming completely irrelevant in a world that doesn't care in the least bit about leaving you behind. You will be 'canceled' soon. Very soon...unless you find your Story."

"Okay...um...I appreciate the offer, but I'm really not sure what you want me to do exactly. How do I find my Story?"

"You must leave the City of Dreams and enter into the Realms of Reality."

"Look. I don't know what that means. It seems to me like I'm in a dream at this very moment trying to understand what the hell you're saying to me."

"Let me be clear then: You've lost your focus and you're experiencing an identity crisis right now, at this very moment. Of course, you're not alone in this regard because your entire industry is experiencing the very same identity crisis. In fact, your country is also experiencing an identity crisis. Your whole modern world is undergoing a crisis of identity so massive in scale that nothing like it has ever been experienced before."

Now, I really was feeling the impact of the cocktail I must have made myself earlier that evening! But the Voice at the other end of the line was unrelenting in its pursuit of me:

"Are you there? Are you there, pal?"

"Look. I'm not one for conspiracy theories and all of that. I'm just a sales guy."

"Dude. I'm gonna hang up now if you don't start paying attention. Except you don't want me to hang up. Because when I hang up *this* time, I will *not* call you again."

I wanted to say, "I think that would probably be okay with me."

But instead, I said, "Okay, how can I help you?"

I just couldn't blow him off. Not this time. I've been blown off before, and I kind of felt sorry for this Voice at the other end of the line pretending to be the future me. Something was drawing me to the Voice. Was it pity? No. Compassion? Hell no. Was it fear? Maybe. *If what the Voice is saying is true, and I'm on my way to irrelevance...* I shuddered at the thought.

Maybe the Voice was on to something here. I've feared being irrelevant for quite some time, actually. My competitors seemed to be gaining relevance while I was not. Even in areas where I was winning, it seemed as if I might start losing. *I hate to lose. I don't want to lose.* I decided to pay attention to the Voice, for just a little while longer.

The Voice continued:

"You need to find your Unique, Authentic Winning Story."

"My Unique, Authentic Winning Story?"

"Yes. The only way forward for you is to find your Unique, Authentic Winning Story. I call it UAWS for short."

"How do I do that?"

"Like I said, you need to..."

"Cut the bullshit. Just give it to me straight."

"Okay, fine. First, you need to find out who your ideal client is and what that person wants or needs. Then you need to create unique value for that particular human being in an authentic way that's true to yourself. Finally, you need to do this in such a way that you win in business without losing in life. Only then can you feel fulfilled in your career and discover your Unique, Authentic Winning Story."

"Look. I've heard something like that many times before, and I've spent my entire career doing exactly that. You're not telling me anything new here."

Just as I was arguing with the Voice, I received an email notifying me that I had lost another sale to someone with a better "story."

"Okay, fine. I'm in."

"You're in?"

"Yes. I want to find my Unique, Authentic Winning Story. What am I supposed to do next?"

"I want you to go in another direction."

"Which direction is that?"

"I'd like you to go on a little adventure with me."

"Sounds interesting."

"It is."

But I was still a little unclear, and I wanted to negotiate for more. "What about your previous offer of 'never losing a sale' if I pay attention to you? Does that offer still apply?"

"You remember that offer?"

"Yes."

"I'm sorry for your loss."

"Excuse me?"

"No, that offer doesn't apply anymore. I never make the same offer twice. Here's my new offer:

"Option 1: Remain in the City of Dreams and become irrelevant, always wondering what would have happened if you had followed my Voice.

"Option 2: Become a StorySeller and embark on an adventure with me through the Realms of Reality. If you make it all the way through to the end, you'll find your Unique, Authentic Winning Story. You'll experience success and freedom beyond your wildest imagination."

"Okay."

"Okay?"

"Yes, okay. Let's do this thing."

Just like that, I agreed to leave my beloved City of Dreams, follow the Voice of my future self, and go on a whimsical, fantastical adventure through the Realms of Reality.

Many would say that my fate was completely doomed from the start or that my destination wasn't worth the danger it took to get there.

Many would say that the characters I met were dubious and that in meeting them, I would become a dubious character myself.

Some would even say that I learned the wrong lessons or that I didn't learn any lessons at all.

But I'll let you, the Reader, draw your own conclusions.

As for my perspective on the matter? This is my story, and I'm sticking to it.

PART I

The Adventure

CHAPTER 1

The Nine Realms of Reality

I WAS BORN IN THE CITY OF DREAMS, WHERE MONEY TALKS AND everything else just walks. Or runs away. Or simply gets ignored and relegated to the sidelines of insignificance. I did not want to be insignificant. I wanted to *matter*. I wanted to *make a difference*. And yes, I wanted to *make money*. So I became a salesman at a very young age. But I didn't start out that way.

At the age of fifteen, I wanted to change the world, so I took an exam that gave me enough college credit to enter law school. I figured I could become a lawyer by twenty, the president of the United States by thirty-five, and the solver of all the world's problems by forty. Then I could retire and spend the rest of my life as a gardener, like the Roman emperor Diocletian.

But life got in the way and my plans changed. I dropped out of law school at sixteen and went into business instead. I dabbled in the financial market for a few years, then in the real estate market at the age of twenty, and in the mortgage market shortly thereafter. I achieved success. I breathed success. I taught success. Until I didn't.

When the housing and financial markets crashed, my business and my business partnerships also crashed. It was like watching a car get smashed up in slow motion. While I was in it with loved ones. While I was trying to stop it. Knowing I couldn't.

I was in business with friends and family, and those relationships collapsed when the business collapsed. Some of those relationships recovered and are stronger now than ever before. Some of those relationships never recovered and most likely never will.

The next decade of my life I spent rebuilding my broken business, on my own. In those years, I enjoyed the splendid spoils of success once again, and I experienced the deep wounds of failure over and over again. I don't think my experiences were all that different from any other modern-day salesman. But when I turned forty, something inside of me changed, or switched on, or switched off...I can't really say.

All I can say is that I became mournful and sad, and thought about death...a lot. I didn't want to die. I just wondered what would happen if I did die. I wondered if my life mattered or if the success I had achieved was worth the pain that it took to achieve it. I wondered if anyone would remember me beyond those who were closest to me.

That was the nature of my reality when I was told by the Voice of my future self that I was living in a dream world and that I had one more chance to be the person I thought I was meant to be. I wanted to believe the Voice. I wanted to believe that I could somehow wake up from my Dream and experience a Reality that was more fulfilling or simply less sad than the one I had become accustomed to.

That's why I followed the Voice toward what it called the Realms of Reality. The Voice led me to a green pasture beside a still lake. The lake was surrounded by majestic mountains robed in evergreen forests and crowned with glimmering peaks of snow. The snow at the top of the mountains melted into cascading rivers and waterfalls that hemmed the mountains as they flowed into the lake. The water in the lake sparkled like a sea of diamonds underneath the shadow of the regal mountains that surrounded it. It was as if the mountains were standing sentry, guarding us, protecting us from whatever lay beyond them.

It was in that meadow, surrounded by mountains, that I laid down for a while and rested, impervious to the outside world. The air was clean and smelled crisp like fall. All was quiet except for the sound of the gentle breeze as it whispered softly across the lake.

The process of resting was new to me. I had been on the go for so long. For many years of my life I had worked long hours—day after day, week after week, month after month, until the months became years and the years turned into decades.

Decades of hard work. Decades of getting rejected by people who I thought had no good reason to reject me. Decades of reinventing myself each morning and hoping the reinvented version of myself would somehow click with the market. Decades of making money and losing money and having countless conversations about making and losing money.

I had spent so many years working under the shadow of Superficial Towers of Success in the City of Dreams that I had no idea an alternate Reality even existed. The buildings in the city were massive, but the people who lived and worked inside of them were small. They were small-minded and small-hearted: shadows of what they could have been. And I was one of them. I was a shadow, living in the shadow of other people's Reality.

All those years of living in the City of Dreams and working under the shadow of Superficial Towers of Success had worn me down so much that yes, I rested when the Voice invited me to rest. And yes, it felt good to rest! The Voice and I had many conversations during that rest, and I'll tell you about them sometime.

Alas, we cannot rest forever or else boredom will turn our restfulness into restlessness. So I got up from my rest and asked the Voice a simple question: "What's next for me?"

The Voice replied, "It's time for you to walk through the Gate."

And with that, the Voice guided me through a pathway to what appeared to be a large Gate leading out of the green meadow where we had been resting. The Gate was massive and tall, as if reaching up to heaven, yet narrow and crooked as if reaching down to hell. It was wrapped with thorns and roses all around. I felt as though the Gate was custom-designed to simultaneously entice and repel people like me.

"This is where I leave you," said the Voice. "I can only lead you to the Gate of the Realms of Reality; you yourself must walk through it. You must use your intuition to find your way through the Realms and discover your Unique, Authentic Winning Story. At the end of your journey, you will have either discovered your Story or died trying."

"That's grim."

"That's Reality."

"And what if I don't want to walk through the Gate?"

"Don't you think that question was asked and answered already?"

"I'm not sure what you mean."

"You're stalling."

"I'm trying to get clarity."

"I can't give you clarity. Nobody can. You must experience the Journey through the Realms of Reality. Only then can you find the clarity you seek."

"I thought the point was to find my 'Unique, Authentic Winning Story.'"

"It is."

I could tell this conversation was going nowhere. So I shrugged, bid the Voice goodbye, and walked through the Gate, cutting my hand on a thorn. I was so focused on my cut that I forgot to delight myself with the fragrance of the beautiful roses.

What greeted me on the other side of the Gate was a loud, bustling city with people shouting at one another and everyone around me clamoring for attention. Whose attention? I just don't know. But the noise level was simply staggering. Unbearable. Unconscionable. *This is Reality?*

Then a woman wearing a see-through plastic mask came running at me. I ducked. She tackled me. I struggled to get away from her. Her stench was ghastly. I gagged. She lunged at me again. She was carrying a see-through plastic Story that matched her see-through ugly mask. Her Story had razor-sharp edges that seemed as if they could cut right through me. It was titled, "Lies and Distortions Disguised as Truth: How to Be Obnoxious Like Me and Blame Everyone Else for Your Problems."

She tried to smack me with her Story as if attempting to cut me to pieces. I didn't want to get smacked or cut to pieces, especially not by someone who looked and smelled like her. So I backed off as best I could and ran as fast as I could.

I ran right into the arms of another woman wearing a see-through plastic mask, carrying a see-through plastic Story. Only this ugly woman was an ugly man. The masks these people wore were hideous, distorting their faces and covering up their humanity, giving the illusion that they all looked the same. Their see-through plastic Stories had different titles, but the designs and shapes were the same, with razor-sharp edges. Worst of all, the people and their Stories smelled disgusting.

I gagged again, backed off, and ran. I found an opening through the crowd and made my way through it. I managed to find a quiet spot to catch my breath. I looked around a bit and noticed that I was in a large square in the middle of a modern-looking city. I saw stone buildings that looked like temples tucked in between glass-covered skyscrapers of all shapes and sizes.

The square was magnificently laid out. The radiant reflections of the beautiful buildings surrounding it danced in the sunlight. The buildings sang songs of the unique genius of the various architects who had designed them as their reflections flickered throughout the square in what seemed like a carefully choreographed dance. But here inside the square, in the midst of all this incredible beauty, were nasty, ugly people, running around, smacking one another with their see-through plastic Stories.

They wore name tags labeled with flowers, but the Stories they carried were literally filled with shit. Bullshit, their shit, and fifty flavors of shit that I had never heard of before in any of my prior travels.

The woman who initially lunged at me labeled herself as a "lotus," but the shit she had oozing out of her Story was so gross and vile that the stench made me vomit. I still gag every time I think of her, lunging at me with her epic Story filled with shit.

As I was dodging the woman and the others who followed her, I thought to myself, *What have I gotten myself into? I should have never followed that crazy Voice in my head. What was I thinking, coming here to this...this...this place?*

Then I noticed a bright sign towering above me that read, "The Square of Modern Marketing." *Well, that explains it.* These people running around the square must be trying to gain attention for themselves and their Stories. *But why were they wearing such* ugly *masks? And why did they use shit for Story-filler when so many other viable options were available?* Then it dawned on me. *These people must seem extra nasty to me because I'm in a new, mythical world. But wasn't this world supposed to be the Realms of Reality?*

As I was trying to make sense of my new surroundings, my eyes caught hold of a sign at the entrance to one of the buildings across the square. It read, "StorySeller Orientation."

It seemed as though it would probably be a good idea for me to start my Journey there and get "oriented." I strategically mapped a path through the crowd and made it safely to the other side of the square.

I was met at the Orientation building by a woman with beautiful honey-brown eyes and an adorable smile. Her face was not covered by an ugly mask. She serenaded me with her angelic greeting: "Hi there!"

I tried to think of a clever response, but all I could manage was, "Uh, hello."

She gracefully continued in a singsong voice, "Come on in. We've been expecting you."

"You've been expecting me?"

"Yes, we have, for quite some time now! I see you finally made it. Orientation is right through those doors. But first, a shower."

She cheerfully pointed to a locker room down the hall and instructed me to make my way directly to the meeting room once I cleaned up. I thanked her and followed her instructions, making a mental note to go back and talk to her at some point, after my shower...after my orientation...maybe before dinner? I was getting hungry. Dinner and drinks sounded nice right about now.

After my thorough shower, I got dressed and doused myself with the cologne that was sitting on the counter, which was my favorite, coincidentally. I spruced up my hair and smiled in the mirror for the cameras, ready to take on the world once again. So I did, sort of.

I made my grand entrance by clumsily stumbling into the room, after tripping over a small garbage can by the doorway. I looked up sheepishly, wondering if anyone had noticed. Everywhere I looked were beautiful people, their faces uncovered. My heart skipped a beat. The instructor at the front of the room acknowledged me as I entered: "Hi there!"

"Hello. Sorry, I didn't mean to interrupt you."

"No apology necessary. We were just getting started. These are your fellow StorySellers, and I'm your instructor. You can call me The Chairman. Now, please take your seat; we've reserved a spot for you."

He motioned for me to sit down near the front of the room. As I made my way toward my seat, my fellow classmates looked me up and down, checking me out. Some of them sneered at me while others appeared indifferent.

As I sat down, I caught the eye of the person sitting next to me. She looked quite stunning and supersmart (as if people can look smart). Also, confident and intimidating. So I looked away, not knowing what to make of her just yet.

As for The Chairman, he was a jovial old man who looked like a modern version of Santa Claus without the long white beard. He had jolly mannerisms, an infectious smile, and a big round belly. He waved his hands wildly when he spoke, and his jokes were hilarious. I'll tell you about them sometime.

The Chairman didn't wear a suit. Perhaps he had concluded that suits were too old-fashioned. Actually, I take that back. He did wear a suit. It was a bright purple athletic jumpsuit, with neon yellow stripes down the shoulders and arms. I guess that's what the cool kids were wearing these days. Except The Chairman wasn't a kid. He was a successful businessman who should have looked like a successful businessman, except that he didn't...or maybe he did. *Weird.*

He pointed to a large map on the wall and started explaining something that seemed important, so I decided to pay attention.

"These are the Nine Realms of Reality," he informed us. "You've each been given your own map, which you will use to navigate your way through the Realms, fulfill your mission, and find your Unique, Authentic Winning Story (UAWS for short)."

I glanced down at the table and saw my map. I read the titles of each of the Realms, as well as a description of what appeared to be a quest or mission associated with each Realm:

1. **The Arena of Warriors:** Enter at your own peril and win the Race if you want to leave alive.

2. **The Isle of Explorers:** Outwit the Sea Monster and help us retrieve our Treasure, or die trying.

3. **The Society of Magicians:** Decipher the Magic Formula of Success and defeat the Evil Sorcerer, or we'll explode you into oblivion.

4. **The Kingdom of Rulers:** Help us tame the Chaos in our kingdom before your Contract runs out, or we'll banish you forever.

5. **The Club of Comedians:** Make us laugh and entertain us, or we'll tell the entire world how utterly boring and uncool you are.

6. **The Community of Friendly Neighbors:** Protect us from the Outsiders who seek to harm us, or we'll "cancel" you and treat you like an Outsider.

7. **The Studio of Artists:** Chisel away with us at the Imperfect until it becomes Magnificent, or fade away in our Prison of Insignificance.

8. **The Academy of Scholars:** Help us find the Truth, or remain lost and forgotten on the never-ending Road to Nowhere.

9. **The Battlefield of Rebels:** Free us from our chains, or die as a meaningless failure after living as a meaningless loser.

The Chairman advised us that we would find our UAWS only by traveling through all nine Realms and completing all nine quests. He concluded his instructions and asked, "Any questions?"

I had a question. "What about all those nasty people outside in the square? What role do they have to play in all of this?"

"Ah, yes," replied The Chairman. "Those are the Exhibitionists. Everyone here has two choices:

"Option 1: Embark on the Journey of StorySellers through the Nine Realms of Reality; or,

"Option 2: Clamor for Attention as Exhibitionists in the Square of Modern Marketing.

"My best advice to you is to just steer clear of the Exhibitionists! Ignore them. Let them sell their Stories in the way they sell them while you sell your Stories in the way you sell them."

"Got it," I replied awkwardly. "Thanks for the explanation."

But The Chairman wasn't done yet with his speech. He turned to the class. "Each of you has been paired with a Worthy Rival. Of course, your primary mission is to complete the nine quests in each of the Nine Realms so that you can find your Unique, Authentic Winning Story. Your secondary mission is to beat your Worthy Rival along the way."

"What's a Worthy Rival?" someone asked.

The Chairman replied by putting on a baseball cap, wearing it backwards. He then crouched down, jutted out his hands, and transformed himself into a rapper:

"Your Worthy Rival is great at what she does, connecting with your audience; the only way to beat her is to put aside your arrogance.

"Your Worthy Rival mesmerizes Clients while you look away, but you can win them back by leveling up without delay.

"Your Worthy Rival's gonna win unless you take her seriously; if you wanna win, show up quick and more strategically."

He paused for effect. We looked back at him, faces blank, slightly confused. We waited for him to continue his rap song. Instead, he grinned mischievously, took off his baseball cap, and put on the soundtrack to *Rocky*, the epic movie. You know, the song that plays in the background when Rocky snatches victory from the jaws of defeat. The Chairman got behind a podium at the front of the room, stood up straight, put on some reading glasses, and transformed himself into a great orator. He then launched into a heroic speech:

"Go on, my fellow StorySellers. Embark on your Journey through the Realms of Reality with Courage, and emerge as Victors!

"StorySellers look in the mirror and remember their truest selves, while Exhibitionists look in the mirror and refuse to see what's right in front of them.

"StorySellers focus on achieving Victory, while Exhibitionists focus on all the reasons why Victory is hard to achieve.

"StorySellers actually achieve Victory without complaining about the effort, while Exhibitionists wallow in Defeat, spending all their effort complaining.

"StorySellers embrace life with no apology, while Exhibitionists waste life waiting for an apology.

"StorySellers help others generously although they're under no obligation, while Exhibitionists rely on the generosity of others as though they're owed an obligation.

"StorySellers sell themselves and others the best version of themselves, while Exhibitionists exhibit to themselves and others the worst version of themselves.

"We do not belong to the tribe of Exhibitionists. We belong to the tribe of StorySellers: A tribe of thinkers and poets and writers. A tribe of kings and queens and conquerors. A tribe of creators and adventurers and explorers. A tribe of people who have known similar pains, sorrows, and failures. People who, despite their pains, sorrows, and failures, rose up to create their best work and to sell it to us when we needed it most.

"StorySellers like Winston Churchill, who sold his country the best version of itself in what seemed to be its most challenging moment. Churchill was sixty-six years old when he created his best work. When he urged his fellow citizens to aim for victory at all costs, victory in spite of all terror, victory, however long and hard the road may be.

"StorySellers like Dr. Martin Luther King Jr., who sold his country the best version of itself in what seemed to be one of its most challenging moments. In moments like this, he'd probably encourage you to shine your light and sell your dream to a world that desperately needs it.

"StorySellers like Maya Angelou, who reminded us why the caged bird sings and that there is no greater agony than bearing the untold Story inside of us."

"These were the StorySellers of yesterday who came before us, who paved the way for us to become the StorySellers of today. 'Find your Unique, Authentic Winning Story,' they beckon to you now. 'Show us how our fights were not fought in vain and how you built upon our good work. Read to us now your chapter in the epic story of humanity. Show us how you journeyed through the Realms of Reality and emerged as Victors!'

"Heed their call to adventure. Consider yourself summoned. And what may seem to be the most challenging moments along your Journey may just yet be the very moments you find your Story and become the Victors you were born to be."

I glanced around the quiet room. Then the applause started quietly with the mesmerizing woman sitting next to me. It grew and grew and grew until the whole room was roaring with applause and was overtaken in a standing ovation for the great orator before us.

I stood up and started clapping too. I wasn't sure whether we were applauding The Chairman's brilliant speech or cheering the end of a long-winded tirade against the nasty Exhibitionists who first greeted us in this strange land.

Either way, I was happy to be standing and joining in this applause, if for no other reason than the realization that I had somehow managed to join a group of people who seemed to be sort of like me. We were fellow StorySellers embarking on an epic adventure together through the Nine Realms of Reality.

Little did I know that we would laugh our way through it, cry our way through it, and sing our way through it. Or that some of us would not even make it past the first Realm, let alone all nine of the Realms.

Little did I know that it would be a culinary adventure, a business adventure, and a spiritual adventure. Or that it would be dangerous and fun, mythical and mystical, entertaining and educational...all at the same time.

Little did I know that the characters I'd meet would purify me, edify me, and energize me. Or that the places they'd take me would fascinate me, dazzle me, and delight me.

But, alas, I don't want to spoil the story for you at such an early stage!

CHAPTER 2

The Arena of Warriors

THE MISSION:

Enter at your own peril and win the Race...if you want to leave alive.

I soon found myself in the Arena of Warriors, stand-ing on the shoulders of the Victors who came before me. But first, let me tell you how I got there... Following The Chairman's rousing speech, my fellow StorySellers and I were led through a long, maze-like corridor for what seemed like a mile or so until we spilled out into a gigantic outdoor arena. We heard a fight song playing on the loudspeakers, and the sign at the entrance displayed its lyrics:

You are the Warriors, the Victors in the Arena.

*May Victory rain down on you from the
goddess Athena.*

You are the Fighters, and you'll fight unto the death

*For Truth and Love and Honor,
until your dying breath.*

*You are the Guardians, the ones who
protect the Realm*

*From Enemies and Monsters
who seek to overwhelm.*

*You are the Champions who champion
noble causes,*

*Even when others try to keep you down
with chains and losses.*

You are the Heroes, in every generation,

From every race and creed, in every nation.

*May Victory rain down on you
from the goddess Athena*

You are the Warriors, the Victors in the Arena.

I could feel goosebumps running up my spine as adrenaline coursed through my veins. The excitement I felt as I entered into the Arena transported me back to my childhood and the times when I had imagined myself to be a great Hero. The Arena resembled a scene out of a movie set in the most ancient of times. There were chariots racing around, creating clouds of blinding dust in their wake.

The Chairman handed us all glasses to shield our eyes and so we could better see inside the Arena. Each pair of glasses was labeled uniquely. Some labels said, "Inventor of Categories" and "Creator of Synergy." It was as if we were each wearing our own name brands. My name brand was simply my name, though.

"The glasses are the perspective with which you see things in the Arena," The Chairman instructed us. When I asked why my glasses were labeled with only my name and not a "cool" brand like the others, The Chairman replied that some people's names are worth more to them than anything else. "You are one such person," he informed me. So then I asked, "Is that a compliment?"

"It could be. Or it could simply signal that you're completely full of yourself and see yourself as better than all the other Warriors you encounter in the Arena. Only Time will tell."

I looked at him with raised eyebrows, disapproving of his answer. He continued to lead us around the Arena, pointing out its sights and sounds. I soon realized there were actually several Arenas connected to one another by long corridors, and we visited a few.

In all the Arenas, I saw distracted Warriors who chased the skirts of their Worthy Rivals and others who played with their swords, pretending they were larger than they actually were. I saw amateur Warriors who shot blanks and professionals who hit their targets with precision. I decided to give it a shot in an Arena called Family. My three shots hit their marks as masterfully as Cupid hits his marks on Valentine's Day.

In the Arena of Politics, I saw weak and arrogant Warriors who acted like cowards and beasts. Then I saw courageous and noble Warriors who were stronger and more honorable than the beasts who fought them. In the Arena of Business, I saw silly Warriors who won silly contests and serious contests that even the most serious Warriors could not win.

But of all the contests in all the Arenas, the Chariot Races of Business seemed to me the most thrilling. That's where most of the Victors of my generation were created. The Victors of the Chariot Races vanquished lesser men, lesser women, lesser people. They were lauded and applauded, idolized and adored. I wanted more than anything else to be like them. I felt ready to vanquish my competitors, and I wanted everyone to see me as I did so. Especially *her*.

My Worthy Rival, the mesmerizing woman who sat next to me during Orientation, had apparently decided that the Chariot

Races of Business were her thing as well. She wasn't distracted by the other Arenas, where frivolous people often played frivolous games. She knew that the Great Contest was looming in the distance, and she was ready to go the distance. As was I. Or so I thought.

The first thing I did was stand on the shoulders of the Victors who came before me, hoping to see what they saw, and even more. I studied the Races, the Arena, and all my competitors. I watched them as they whizzed by me, creating clouds of dust in their wake. I knew I was destined to race alongside them and claim my Victory.

I began pursuing my destiny with the same grace with which I'd entered the Orientation room—my feet slipped and I stumbled clumsily into the Arena, landing facedown. Undaunted, I got up, brushed myself off, and ran to the Master Charioteer. I asked him to grant me my chariot. He asked whether I wanted to apprentice under another Charioteer before going out on my own. I quickly replied, "No. I got this."

He shrugged and gave me a chariot, and then I was off to the Races. The first race I entered was really no contest at all. I handily won, leaving my competitors in the dust. Looking back at that moment, I can't help but realize how large a role luck and timing played in that first victory. Even someone without any experience, like me, can get lucky every now and again.

My Worthy Rival entered the competition in the second race. As she made her grand entrance into the Arena, she removed her glasses and looked directly at the crowd gathered in the stands.

Her eyes were black and soulless, piercing me with dread even though she never looked directly at me. Her nostrils flared as her jet-black hair blew in the wind, forming a trail of intimidation behind her. She was perfectly poised, unshakably confident, and ravishingly gorgeous. Her outfit accentuated the seductive curves of her perfectly toned body. The crowd went wild with admiration, and I cowered like a pitiful fool.

On her heels, another Competitor entered the Arena from seemingly nowhere. He too was perfectly poised, unshakably confident, and ravishingly gorgeous. He wore no shirt, and his lack of clothing accentuated the seductive curves of his perfectly toned chest. He was like an Adonis chasing after *my* Worthy Rival. Again, the crowd went wild with admiration, and I cowered like a pitiful fool.

The Adonis's reputation preceded his grand entrance like a parade of trumpets heralding the arrival of an emperor. His loyal worshippers filled the Arena with a chorus of praises, while my Worthy Rival effortlessly rallied half the crowd to chant her praises in response. The chorus of the crowd was so compelling that I bizarrely felt myself wanting to join in their worship of the god and goddess who had graced the Arena with their presence.

Yet I wanted to disappear as well. I was a speck of dust just waiting for the wheels of their chariots to blow me away into oblivion. I was ready to give up my shaky, misguided desire for Victory right then and there.

As my shame and jealousy subsided, however, I began to fume. *How could not even a single person in this Arena notice me? My Worthy Rival didn't even notice me! I deserved to be noticed. I would make them notice me, and I would make them regret the day they even entered this Arena. My Arena.*

When the trumpet sounded and the Race began, I took off like a demon out of Hell, quickly gaining the lead. The wind was blowing through my hair, and I wondered how intimidating I must be in that moment to my Worthy Rival and the Adonis chasing after her. My nostrils flared and I began to look at my own body, which was certain to be ravishing to the eyes of anyone lucky enough to catch a glimpse.

I marveled at how chiseled and sexy I must have looked at this very moment, as I was firmly in the lead on my way to certain Victory. Why not rip off my shirt and remove my glasses in one graceful move? I was unstoppable. Unbeatable. Untouchable. I had graced this Arena with my presence, and soon enough everyone would be chanting my praises while my Worthy Rival and her Adonis cowered in shame like pitiful fools. I rounded the corner, making my way toward final Victory.

Then quite suddenly, I began to hear a swooshing sound, whirring louder with each passing second. Without my permission, the Winds of Change blew overhead, altering the entire climate and atmosphere of the Arena. I choked. I couldn't manage to adjust my chariot quickly enough because I was so busy trying to flex my muscles and rip off my shirt for the crowd.

That's all it took for the Adonis and his conniving witch to overtake me. They whizzed past me, blinding me with the dust kicked up from their chariots. The Adonis clipped my chariot wheels with his own, and my Worthy Rival shouted condescendingly to me, "Thanks for playing, champ."

My chariot flew into the air and then crashed to the ground, shattering into a million little pieces. I trailed right behind it, crashing facedown into the dust, my ego shattering into a million little pieces.

The crowd didn't even notice my demise, as they remained focused on my Worthy Rival and the Adonis who was chasing her. She ended up winning the Race, but that's her Story.

As for my Story, I feared that it would end before it even began, with my face planted in the dust, here in this Arena of Warriors. After the Race, I retreated into the bathroom and tended to my physical and emotional wounds. At the most inopportune time, just as I was taking a piss, The Chairman walked in, looked at me, and said,

"I see you only use one hand to hold it. What a shame. The best of us need to use both hands."

I could feel my face turning red. I looked down. He chuckled and admonished me.

"Come on. Stop taking yourself so seriously. You lost one Race. There will be others. We're having dinner in the Winner's Club later on. Why don't you join us?"

I stuttered a bit and asked why I should want to do that, given that I hadn't won any victories today. I told him I wasn't a fan of giving out trophies for effort, and I wasn't in the mood to celebrate other people's success. He replied that a man who can't lose gracefully is no man at all, and that the first step to becoming a Victor is to understand what losing feels like.

He instructed me: "Harness the feelings you're feeling right now in this instant and toss them into the fire of Passion that burns inside you. Every time you lose, harness that feeling and turn it into fuel. Then heap that fuel into your fire of Passion. Fan the flames of that fire and keep on fueling it until it burns so hot that you cannot contain it any longer. In this manner, your Passion will grow until it reaches the temperature necessary to burn true and will never burn out regardless of the circumstance. Otherwise, each Victory you achieve will be just a flash in the pan. Each Loss will push you to the edge of being a has-been who only pretends at Victory."

I nodded, though I still was unconvinced. I agreed to meet him in the Winner's Club later that evening.

Happily, I entered the Winner's Club without a repeat performance of the trash can incident. I looked up to see walls lined with portraits of Victors who had won gloriously in the Arena. I saw captains of industry who managed to consistently turn out profits while leading their companies to greatness. I saw world leaders who helped humanity achieve Victory through the darkest of times. I saw saints who were larger than life, and sinners who seized every opportunity in life. I saw all kinds of people from my generation and those before it. The one thing these Victors had in common was that they had won against all odds.

I wondered how hot their Passion burned and how many Losses had fueled their flames. I concluded that The Chairman was right, and I vowed to return to this Arena as a Victor. I started making plans to come back the next day and make my comeback. Just as I was getting lost in the labyrinth of my own thoughts, The Chairman got up to make his speech.

First, he addressed my Worthy Rival, who had earned first place in the Chariot Race. "Congratulations on your well-earned Victory! My best advice to you is to savor it. Enjoy it. But don't ever be comfortable with it. You now have a target on your back, and others will come gunning for you. Your Victory will be short-lived if you fail to continuously improve your skills or if you slip into a state of comfort."

Then he addressed the Adonis, who had come in second place. "You, like the second child of any family, will always feel a need to compete with the one who came ahead of you. Harness that competitive feeling but don't be consumed by it. Otherwise, it will turn into jealousy and your emotions will overtake you. Discipline yourself and practice correctly. Constantly. Courageously. Create your own path to Victory, and Victory can be yours."

Finally, he addressed me because I had apparently come in third place. "You, like the third child in any family, must create your own way so as not to be overshadowed by those who came ahead of you. For this reason, and for your own benefit, I'm removing you from this Arena and setting you on your own path. You will be your own Worthy Rival throughout most of your remaining Journey through the Realms."

I objected, stating my concern that if I was forced to leave the Arena and become my own Worthy Rival, I wouldn't be able to compete for my rightful place in the Great Contest that he had first told us about during Orientation.

He replied that I'd be entered into the Great Contest regardless, as long as I could make it all the way through the remaining Realms and complete all the quests. "The StorySeller's Journey through the Nine Realms is like an infinite game," he instructed. "The objective is to find your Unique, Authentic Winning Story and then help others do the same. The game never ends, and the ones who excel at it leave a legacy. They win at life regardless of whether they win or lose in business.

"On the other hand, the Chariot Race in the Arena is a finite game. If you devote your life to winning the Race at the expense of all else, you risk losing at life regardless of whether you win or lose in business."

Still, I argued with him, thinking myself to be in the right and not quite understanding his meaning. I simply didn't want to leave this Arena, where I felt I belonged. He then reminded me that The Chairman makes the rules. That's why he's The Chairman and I'm not.

Sensing my growing dissatisfaction, he warned me to be careful what I wish for, to pick my battles wisely, and to remember that not everything needs to be a fight.

"You may actually enjoy being your own Worthy Rival and traveling the Nine Realms," he said. "Not everyone's cut out for it because they take their cue from other people. But you, on the other hand, have glasses bearing your own name. You can really make something of yourself and forge your own path."

I paused, thought about what he said, and begrudgingly agreed to give it a shot. He invited me to grab some dinner and said we'd talk about it some more over a glass of scotch. And so we did. The Chairman invited me to sit at his table alongside my Worthy Rival and the Adonis.

We were served hamburgers and fries, which, by the way, were absolutely delicious. I asked for more, and they kept bringing me more. I ate so many fries that day that I began to grow a belly.

Then it dawned on me why The Chairman wore athletic jumpsuits instead of the slim business suits that I had been accustomed to wearing. Unbeknownst to me, my belly would grow several sizes throughout my Journey, but that is another story for another time.

As for this story at this time, I was content to eat my burgers and fries. After dinner, we were served old-fashioned cocktails, Manhattans, and all sorts of drinks I had never heard of. We were then invited to mix our own cocktails.

I created a delicious drink consisting of:

1 part rye whiskey

1 part sweet vermouth

$\frac{1}{2}$ part amaro

$\frac{1}{2}$ part bitter bianco

$\frac{1}{4}$ part maraschino liqueur

$\frac{1}{4}$ part smoky, peaty scotch from Islay in Scotland

2 dashes of Angostura bitters

1 maraschino cherry (garnish)

Combine all ingredients and add ice. Stir together, don't shake. Strain and pour into a coupe glass containing one maraschino cherry. Served straight up.

I called this The StorySeller cocktail, and I drink it quite often, even to this very day.

Throughout the evening, I kept a close eye on my Worthy Rival and her Adonis, studying their every move, wondering when I would make it back to this Arena to reclaim the Victory that they had snatched from me.

The Chairman, perhaps noticing my agitation, quickly introduced me to the Explorer, who would take me to the next Realm. He asked the Explorer to give me a passport so I could enter the next Realm, which he did. It was an odd-looking passport—more of a necklace and charm if you ask me. I'm really not sure why he called it a passport.

Regardless, The Chairman said I could keep my Warrior glasses in case I needed them in the future. He said, "Once a Warrior, always a Warrior." Then he started grilling me with questions.

"What did you learn in this Arena of Warriors?"

"I learned that I must stay focused regardless of the Winds of Change, and that I must adjust my chariot to the Winds whenever they come blowing my way."

"What else did you learn?"

"I learned that I must never underestimate my Worthy Rival or the other competitors in the Arena."

"And what else did you learn?"

I glared at him before answering facetiously, "I learned that not everything needs to be a fight and that I should pick my battles wisely."

"Very good," he answered, ignoring my condescending tone. "In this manner, you must summarize your learnings in each Realm before leaving it. At the end of your Journey, you'll remember those lessons. You'll remember the people you met and the places you visited. Then you'll decide which of those Realms spoke to you the most and where you'd like to make your home. In that Realm, the one that speaks to you the most, you'll find your Unique, Authentic Winning Story."

"Wait. You're not coming with me?"

"No. This is where I leave you."

"But how will I know where to go and how to get there?"

"You still have the map I gave you in Orientation, don't you? Use your intuition. I believe in you. Your Voice believes in you. Now it's time for you to believe in yourself."

I reluctantly nodded my head and asked him when I would be able to return to the Arena. I explained that I very much wanted a rematch in the Chariot Races and that I felt my time here was cut short. The Chairman assured me I would one day, in the not-too-distant future, return to the Arena of Warriors and that I would even spend an entire season of my life here. "But first," he said, "you must learn many things in the other Realms. Most importantly, you must learn how to win even when you lose."

I shrugged at his seemingly cryptic response, bid him farewell, and followed the Explorer, who promised to take me to the next Realm of my Journey.

I had no idea about the unusual characters I'd meet there or the unbelievable stories they'd tell me. I had no clue that I'd cluelessly forget my own value. Or that I'd argue over peanuts.

I had no clue that I'd dine in solitude for what seemed like a hundred years, after finding hidden Treasures that I had lost long ago.

As I continued on my Journey toward the Isle of Explorers, I wondered whether I'd learn in that Realm how to win even when I lose. I wondered whether the lessons I'd learn there would be enough to allow me admittance back into the Arena of Warriors, where I felt I belonged.

I should have heeded The Chairman's earlier warning to be careful what I wished for.

CHAPTER 3

The Isle of Explorers

THE MISSION:

Outwit the Sea Monster and help us retrieve our Treasure...or die trying.

THE EXPLORER TRANSPORTED ME TO AN ISLE OF LIKE-MINDED Explorers who were dissatisfied with life in the other Realms. They had gathered here and formed their own community free from the so-called Civilized Society that drove them away. I heard many conflicting stories about why they had come here and what they were looking for. Here's how one Explorer summarized it for me:

> In the modern age, it all started with the Americans and their shenanigans. They liberated the world, then raided its Treasure, while everyone watched and lost count of the measure.

> The Terrorists attacked and the Capitalists responded. The war raged on and the people desponded.

> Some fool got the idea to build a big wall and said Mexico would pay for it all. When his project failed, his people bailed. They chose an old man and the old man panned. The people objected, and the Rebels grabbed hold. The burnout is real; it's getting so old.

> Viruses spread, supply chains shut down, and Russia attacked while everyone was down.

> China stole data, denying they did, but everyone knew that they did and they hid.

> Men became women and women became men. Some became persons and some forgot they were humans.

> Some trashed the environment while others blamed the trash for the destruction of humanity and their own shortage of cash.

The climate suffered; the people sputtered. Business owners struggled; employees muttered.

Blacks turned on Whites after Whites snuffed out their lights. Asians and Caucasians were persecuted; Arabs and Jews were executed. Hispanics created music but then got deported.

Europeans fought; everyone was distraught. North America went south and South America went north.

Everyone lost their identity in those dark ages of Humanity. Humans became beasts and the beasts ruled Earth. So some built spaceships and tried to leave Earth.

The people slurred, they yelled, they hurt. But no one was listening 'cause they all were hollering. The noise in the place got really obnoxious, and the toxic air got really noxious.

Two percent of the population controlled one hundred percent of the conversation! The rest objected. They texted. But they had no clue what to do.

Some hid in corners, blaming the foreigners. Some blamed the rich and said they should pay, which wasn't so smart because they were already paying the way.

Inflation set in after money dropped in by the buckets and liters from clueless smart leaders.

Then people like me said, "We're out! That's enough! Let's leave this place now, straight away, at once!"

We became Explorers and we're searching for a way to get back our Treasure that was taken away.

It's ours, it's mine, it's yours. It belongs to us. There's nothing to discuss.

We're going to find it and take it and share it. Here's a carrot.

I took his carrot and started munching. I was hungry for something different, so I decided to join him and his friends on their Journey.

My new friends and I met a brilliant salesman who understood our needs. He sold us a map that he promised would help us navigate the Blue Ocean of Life and Business. He pointed out that there were actually two oceans that we could navigate, but he didn't recommend the Red Ocean.

He explained: "The Great Sea Monster lives in the Red Ocean and has a reputation of devouring any Explorer who tries to pass without his permission. Even the Explorers who receive the Great Sea Monster's blessing have to tread carefully because he is prone to mood swings of the most violent nature. The Red Ocean is red because of all the blood in the water from the Great Sea Monster's many victims."

He then told us how the Great Sea Monster wasn't the only predator in those red waters. The Red Ocean was apparently filled with competing lesser Sea Monsters, each trying to outdo the other, and each trying to control the Red Ocean. The Red Ocean was known to contain many Treasures, but access to those Treasures was denied by the plethora of Sea Monsters who swam there. They claimed their territory and defended it fiercely. They created Monopolies of Wealth for themselves and tore apart anyone who tried to stop them.

"The Blue Ocean," he informed us, "has very few predators and is more suitable for exploration. It's sailed only by enterprising entrepreneurs and people who are always keen on lowering taxes. The water in the Blue Ocean is crystal clear, and the Treasures are often hidden in plain sight. Even so, the Treasures are only accessible to people who think differently and are willing to help each other. Unlike the Red Ocean, there are no Sea Monsters who seek to divide and conquer. In fact, cooperation among Explorers who sail the Blue Ocean is very much encouraged, as are any and all forms of creativity."

He went on to explain that the brave Explorers who explored the Blue Ocean of Life and Business didn't complain about the Sea Monster and all the blood in his Red Ocean. They didn't complain about how unfair the world is, and how everybody hates them, and how nobody loves them. They didn't feel entitled to any handouts and they only wanted to explore the Blue Ocean of Life and Business in peace. Often alone. Sometimes together. Always with good food and drink.

And with that, the brilliant salesman took us to his favorite restaurant on the side of the Isle of Explorers where they served fried fish and grilled fish, small fish and big fish, crab and lobster, and even octopus. They served oysters with brine and mussels soaked in white wine. They served baskets of warm bread and chowder. Lots and lots of chowder...from Boston.

Then all of a sudden, in the middle of our meal, my new friends and I got into a very heated argument. We began yelling at each other and throwing food at one another.

"East Coast!" I shouted.

"West Coast!" they shouted back.

"East Coast!" I shouted louder.

"West Coast!" they yelled louder still.

"EAST COAST!" I screamed at the top of my lungs.

"WEST COAST!" they screamed back, shattering glasses and smashing down plates.

We hadn't even begun drinking yet because it was only 11:00 a.m. local time. Not that I haven't had my share of 11:00 a.m. cocktails, mind you, but I digress. So many stories, so little time!

Anyhow, back to the argument. What was it about? Ah, yes. Oysters. We were arguing the merits of West Coast oysters versus East Coast oysters. My friends leaned west, and I leaned east. We were super-passionate about our positions and decided to order some drinks to help us decide.

So the Germans served us beer while the Greeks served us ouzo. Then the Lebanese served us arak, which tasted like ouzo. The Brazilians served us caipirinhas, and the Japanese served us sake. Then the Colombians joined us, and we all had coffee. We drank Turkish coffee, which was similar to Greek coffee, and then Cuban coffee with lots of sugar. We had Italian espresso and American lattes, served with even more sugar. We talked and talked about our upcoming Journey and ate and drank as if we were in a British tourney.

If you ever have a chance to drink Greek ouzo or Lebanese arak, always remember to mix it with water. The ratio is one part arak and two parts water. The drink turns milky and tastes like licorice. It pairs really well with fish and seafood. Some of my friends forgot to mix their drink with water, and the state of their drunkenness that followed was quite disastrous for them.

As for me, I stuck with Brazilian caipirinhas because those also pair well with fish and seafood, and really anything and everything. For the best caipirinha, simply muddle a juicy lime with two spoonfuls of sugar. Then fill up the glass with crushed ice and pour cachaça to the rim. Dump the mixture into a shaker and then shake. Pour it back into the glass and your world will quake!

The lovely morning became a lovely afternoon, and the lovely afternoon became an epic evening. For it was there, on the shores of the Blue Ocean, that my friends and I forgot our worries and set aside our troubles for another day. The salt water from the breeze became as sweet as sugar when it touched our lips.

As we got drunk that day on our friendship and made epic plans for our business, we prepared our magnificent ship to sail across the Blue Ocean.

For *that*, my friend, is what Explorers do. They sail in magnificent ships to magnificent places, eating and drinking magnificently. Now I was an Explorer among Explorers, going to find my Treasure on the Blue Ocean of Life and Business.

We set sail in our ship and explored the Blue Ocean, finding Treasures in the most unlikely of places. We created unique value for others and did things for them that none of our competitors were doing. We were impervious to the competitive Sea Monsters, who continued battling it out among each other in the Red Ocean.

Then on one particular expedition while sailing the Blue Ocean of Life and Business, we found massive amounts of Treasure. It all started when we realized that Explorers need help while searching for their Treasure. So, instead of searching for our own Treasure, like everyone else, we began to help the other Explorers find *their* Treasure. We became so successful in our endeavors that the Explorers we helped were generous enough to share their Treasure with us after we helped them find it.

This resulted in us accumulating lots and lots of hidden Treasure, which we all shared together. Until we didn't. Some of us got greedy. You see, the Treasure we found was called Money and Financial Success. It's the kind of Treasure that makes people go crazy. It stirs up jealousy and hatred and greed. It's never enough, it's often fleeting, and it always takes on a life of its own.

Money and Financial Success in this Realm look like small green Jewels. The interesting thing about these Jewels, however, is that they multiply and grow on their own once you acquire your first million or so. The mission, in most cases for most Explorers, is to find and acquire their first million Jewels. At that point, more options open up, and the Jewels, if handled properly, begin to multiply and grow on their own.

That's why some of us wanted more Treasure. Some of us wanted all the Treasure for themselves. Some of us wanted to go on their own voyage across the Blue Ocean, leaving the rest of us behind. Or, I should say, leaving *me* behind. The friends who had taught me so much were now leaving me. I didn't know why. As they left, a part of me left with them.

As I watched them leave, I wondered, *Was it me? Is there something I did to drive them away? Is there something I can do now to get them to reconsider?* I tried to approach them, but they were not approachable. I tried to negotiate with them, but they were not in the mood to negotiate. I tried to reason with them, but they had their own reasons and had no interest in my reasons. It all started when they made me a ridiculous offer:

"Give us your half of the Treasure," they demanded, "and we'll give you half of what it's worth."

"No thanks," I replied. "I'll give you my half of the Treasure if you give me 100 percent of what it's worth."

They replied, "No thanks. We have billions of Jewels, and you only have a million. In this Realm, when you have billions more

Jewels than everyone else, you get whatever you want, whenever you want, however you want. So we think our offer is a very fair deal, considering you'll end up with at least more than zero Jewels."

I replied, "I'll tell you what. If you think your offer is such a great deal, why don't we reverse it? You give me your half of the Treasure, and I'll give you half of what it's worth."

They quickly replied, "Nah, we'd rather just make your life difficult until you cave in and give us what we want. Most people eventually cave in and give us what we want."

I said, "Nah, I'm not most people."

So I didn't cave, and they didn't stop demanding. We argued on the shores of the Blue Ocean for two full years. All the while, the waves of the Blue Ocean kept washing over us and our Jewels. By the time we disbanded, all of our Jewels had been reduced to peanuts.

And so it came to pass that we parted ways over peanuts instead of multiplying our Jewels many times over. We became islands unto ourselves instead of working together to take the entire island for ourselves.

I've often wondered what could have happened had things gone differently. So I *did* something different. I thought differently. I asked myself different questions. Ridiculous questions: *Did I pick the right partners? When the waves of the Blue Ocean changed, did I adjust accordingly?*

I discovered that nobody can control the waves of the Blue Ocean or the destinations it makes possible to explore. I learned that your Jewels turn into peanuts when you argue on the sidelines of the Blue Ocean instead of seizing every opportunity to explore it. *What would have happened*, I wondered, *if I had just let things go and moved on with my life? Was fighting that particular battle for two years worth the lost opportunities that it cost me in Life and Business?*

I learned that trying to seize an opportunity in Life or Business after it has already passed by is like trying to catch a wild wave of the ocean and force it to stay in place. It's best to quickly move on and acknowledge the reality that the old wave has passed. If you linger too long waiting in vain for it to come back, you'll miss the next wave, and the one after that. Before long, the whole ocean will have washed over you and passed you by, transforming all your Jewels into peanuts.

I discovered that people's needs change, and the unique value I provide must also change in order to remain relevant to them. Otherwise, it's best for me to let them go and for them to let me go, sooner rather than later, and without bitterness. In this way, we can forever preserve our Beloved Memories as they age with us as a fine wine and become even sweeter.

I learned that Explorers value the *experience* of exploring. They don't want to feel trapped by me, or by the Realm, or by other people living in the Realm who make their lives difficult. I learned that Explorers come from every race and creed, and what they value most is their independence to explore without others judging them, or trapping them in a corner, or otherwise hindering them from exploring.

I learned that I could live among the Explorers, and help them explore, and become an Explorer myself. And so I did. I decided to sail across the Blue Ocean of Life and Business on my own. The Chairman, after all, had believed in me. He assured me back when we were dining together in the Winner's Club that I was destined to complete my Journey and become my own Worthy Rival. If The Chairman himself believed in me, why shouldn't I believe in myself?

So I went in another direction; I'm sure you understand. I mapped out a course for myself and set sail across the Blue Ocean of Life and Business. I was surprised no one else had ever sailed this way before. Everyone was going west, but I went east. I found my own stolen Treasure, and I took it and shared it.

But here's the thing: I found more than just the Treasure of Money and Financial Success on that Journey. I found the Treasure of Self-Reliance when I created value on my own, regardless of what others did or failed to do. Self-Reliance became my best friend, and together we discovered the hidden Treasure of Teamwork.

Teamwork only appeared to me after I had spent many days and nights working alone with Self-Reliance. That's because Teamwork values, most of all, people who contribute the best version of themselves to their team. Only those who've met Self-Reliance can do that. Everyone else becomes a drag on the team, and a team is only as strong as its weakest member.

Later in my Journey, I found the hidden Treasures of Gratitude and Lessons Learned. Those hidden Treasures appeared to me only when I saw with my heart and listened with my eyes. "Every experience on the Blue Ocean of Life and Business is a gift,"

Gratitude said to me one day. "And of all the gifts you are given, the Lessons you learn are the most valuable."

My favorite hidden Treasures that I found, though, were Meaning and Joy. They were two little girls about the age of nine, who never seemed to grow older through the millennia of human history. Apparently, they accompany travelers like us, befriending us and causing us to giggle with delight whenever we do meaningful work and create unique value for others.

Meaning had long, wavy hair, which she wore in a ponytail with a big blue bow. She had piercing brown eyes, and I felt that she could see deep into my soul each time she looked at me. One day, I asked her about the meaning of life. She replied, "That's the wrong question, my friend. Instead of asking what's the meaning of life in general, ask what's the meaning of your life in this moment. What are you doing right now to create unique value for yourself and for the people around you? By answering that question, you can figure out the meaning of your life right now."

Her wisdom was beyond her years, and she gave me a book called *Man's Search for Meaning.* It was written by Viktor Frankl, a Holocaust survivor who found Meaning even in the middle of living in a concentration camp.

Joy, on the other hand, had short, curly hair, which was always tousled and messy. She had big blue eyes that caused me to break out into a fit of laughter each time she looked at me. She really gave me the giggles! I still laugh out loud each time I think about her and her sister, who became great friends to me.

All these hidden Treasures I found while searching for the Treasure of Money and Financial Success. To me, the hidden Treasures were more valuable than the original Treasure I had set out to find.

That's why I labeled those hidden Treasures as "My Hidden Treasures." I would guard them with my life, and no one would ever be able to take them away from me.

After I took back My Hidden Treasures, I was ready to party! I returned to that delightful restaurant where the brilliant salesman had taken me. Only this time, I dined in solitude, cherishing My Hidden Treasures, instead of dining with treasured friends.

After dining in solitude for what felt like a hundred years, I realized that I was not alone after all. My Beloved Memories had graced me with a surprise visit. So we ate and drank together as we spoke of days gone by.

In due time, Bitterness crept up and tried to attack us, but I told that nasty witch to leave us alone. My Beloved Memories were *mine*, and I would never let them go, not to Bitterness, or anyone else for that matter.

My Beloved Memories and I enjoyed an epic evening together. We decided to throw ourselves an after-party to cap it off. We made the dubious decision to explore the dozens of establishments that lined the coastal side of the Isle of Explorers where we were dining at the time.

We happened to walk into one particular establishment where our eyes were met by gorgeous belly dancers, swaying their bodies to the exotic beats of Arabic music. I felt as though Aladdin was going to fly in on his magic carpet at any moment. And then he did. Or so it seemed to me.

I glimpsed traces of a little boy in the background, appearing and then disappearing into the skirts of the beautiful dancers. It was as if he was performing some sort of dance of his own. I was so intrigued by the visible and then invisible boy that I tore my eyes away from the beautiful dancers.

That's probably a good thing too, because I feared my wife would somehow find out I was here. And if so, how would I explain to her that I just got here by "accident" and that I was on my way out? Who would believe such a thing?

Regardless, my eyes followed the boy as he weaved his way toward a doorway at the back of the room. I could hear such uproarious laughter coming through the doorway that I was compelled to go and check it out. I wanted to know what all the fuss was about, and I was fascinated by the way the boy made himself visible and then invisible, only to be made visible once again.

I bid my Beloved Memories goodbye and decided to go on another little adventure (I was an Explorer, after all). So I followed the boy and was careful to avert my eyes from the beautiful dancers and their enticements. Please tell my wife, if you see her, that I didn't look. I didn't touch. Nothing happened.

When I walked through the door into the room from which the uproarious laughter was coming, I found myself in the company of children. The children were watching a few of their esteemed colleagues perform all sorts of magic tricks, the likes of which I had never seen before. There were five child magicians in the front of the room disappearing and then reappearing in different parts of the room mere seconds later. *How very strange*, I thought. Then the strangeness became even stranger.

All of a sudden, bowls of sugary candy, boxes of delicious chocolates, and buckets of gelato and ice cream miraculously appeared from nowhere and softly landed in the middle of the room as if delivered by angels. The children roared in delight, and I unashamedly joined them because *who wouldn't want a delicious meal of sugary candy, delicious chocolate, and ice cream delivered straightaway and served to them?*

The boy who led me here then went to the front of the room and whistled so loudly that all the other boys and girls quieted down, myself included.

"Listen," he said. "You ain't seen nothin' yet! If you come with me and join my Society of Magicians, you can eat all the candy and chocolate you want. I'll show you how to disappear and then reappear wherever you want. I'll show you how to perform tricks like you've never seen before."

I must admit that his promise was quite enticing, even to an avowed skeptic like me. I had ceased believing in Magic long ago, and I wondered what the boy's angle was here.

"But wait, there's more," he continued. Then he vanished. He reappeared next to me. "We should invite this guy!" He took my hand in his and then held it up for everyone to see.

Unbeknownst to me, this child was familiar with the Treasures I had found while sailing the Blue Ocean of Life and Business. He recognized my value even though I didn't recognize him. He understood somehow (maybe because he was a Magician) that the natural next progression for me on my Journey was to join his Society of Magicians. So he took my hand and told the children all the reasons why they should invite me along.

The room was quiet as he spoke. The children looked at me funny, and one of them said, "No way! He's an Adult. He can't come."

I was wounded and felt dejected by the response. I was curious to go with them. I wanted to Explore other Realms. It's not as if I *needed* to go with them. Or maybe I did. My intuition told me that it was time for me to visit another Realm and continue on my Journey. Up until now, I had raced my chariot as a Warrior in the Arena, and I had explored the Blue Ocean of Life and Business as an Explorer. It seemed only fitting that I should join the Society of Magicians and make some Magic.

So I asked the children whether I could join them. I asked them nicely, very nicely. They said no, very meanly. Very, *very* meanly. They were being mean to me. I was being nice to them. Each time I asked nicely, they meanly said no. This wasn't fair.

I wanted them to say yes. I *needed* them to say yes. But all they would say was, "No. No. No."

Then I asked them to say no, knowing they'd finally say yes. I began telling them all the reasons why they should say no. I said, "Look. You're 100 percent right. I'm really not sure if this is a good fit. I thought I might be able to help you get back here in case you didn't like the Society of Magicians. I'm an Explorer, after all, and I thought you were too. I thought together we could explore this other Realm and have the freedom to come back here if we want. But I can see now how I had it wrong all along. You're not really Explorers, are you? Perhaps I misunderstood. I'm very sorry."

I got up to leave. *First person to talk loses.* They lost!

"No, wait! What if we do wanna come back here? Are you sure you can help us find the way? Not that we'd *need* you to help us, of course."

And just like that, the children who were mean to me began to believe in me. I had figured out a way to apply the lessons I had learned in this Realm to find out what my fellow Explorers *really, really* want. Which, in this case, was to have options. To be free to come and go as they please. To *explore.*

For *that,* my friend, is what StorySellers do. They find out what their clients *really, really* want and then figure out a way to give it to them. Now I was starting to become a StorySeller among the Explorers, helping my fellow travelers find *their* Treasure on the Blue Ocean of Life and Business.

The next day, we set sail for the mainland where we would join the Society of Magicians. I wondered what Treasures we would find, and what Magic we would create together.

Little did I know that I'd decipher the Magic Formula of Success, or that disappearing and reappearing again wasn't as hard as it looked.

As for the candy? I couldn't have imagined what crazy treats were in store for me at the candy store.

CHAPTER 4

The Society of Magicians

THE MISSION:

Decipher the Magic Formula of Success and defeat the Evil Sorcerer...or we'll explode you into oblivion.

WE ARRIVED AT A PORT ON THE MAINLAND WHERE WE DISEM-
barked our ship and walked straight into a Tunnel of Technology. During my voyage, I had found comfort in hanging out
with a timid little boy and girl who were quiet, like me. We had
shared many moments of blissful silence as we wondered what
the future had in store for us in this new Realm. As we shuffled
off the ship and into the Tunnel, we were struck by the sheer
magnitude of people in this place. It was as if all of humanity
had crowded into this one Tunnel and was going in the exact
same direction, except they weren't. Or were they? *Weird.* We
were greeted by robots who gave us hand sanitizer and sang us a
cheerful song that went like this:

> Welcome to the Tunnel, where Technology is indispensable.
>
> Welcome to Technology, where everything is multidimensional.
>
> Welcome to the Realm of Magic, where Magicians work and play.
>
> Welcome to a brave new world that's reinvented each and
> every day.
>
> Welcome to a universe that's completely out of your control.
>
> Welcome to dashboards that make it seem like you're in
> control.
>
> But never forget this: Nothing is as it seems.
>
> Things that seem confusing may just be amusing.
>
> And things that seem amusing may actually be abusing

Your privacy and sensibility and even your humanity.

Welcome to Technology, where everything is multidimensional.

Welcome to the Tunnel, where Technology is indispensable.

The Tunnel of Technology spilled out into a dreamlike world, where Magic pixie dust filled the air. I saw Magicians who created Jobs and opened Gates, creating Buffets of Wealth across the Realm. They carried small tablets and guarded them more zealously than Moses must have guarded the tablets on which were written the Ten Commandments. These tablets, however, contained different commandments: commandments like "give me directions" or "deliver me a pizza." Commandments that were created by men and women and that made humans seem like gods. Commandments that seemed to make life easier and more complicated, more enjoyable and more stressful all at the same time.

I saw Magicians who traveled through the Realm as deftly as natives travel across the Amazon. Their Magic tablets brought the world to them, and they used their tablets to travel the world. I ogled the Magicians wherever I'd go, and I followed them wherever they'd go. I read their faces like an open book and liked their Stories wherever I'd look. The musk of the Magicians overtook my senses, and I decided to become one of them. So I did. Sort of.

The boy who led me here with the other children introduced me to the Master Magician, who assigned Roles in this Realm.

She stood tall, and her dark skin glistened with glitter underneath her form-fitting dress. Yet, her exotic beauty was somehow understated.

It was almost as if she were a bashful supermodel not wishing to call attention to herself. But her efforts at modesty were unsuccessful. Magic glitter danced around her gorgeous eyes as her melodic voice and flirtatious words enthralled me. I quickly came under her spell.

I felt as though I'd do absolutely anything she asked of me, now and until the end of my days. No matter the cost. No matter the time. No matter the effort. Which is why I'm so grateful that what she asked of me was relatively restrained, at least compared to what it could have been.

The Master Magician informed me that the current project everyone was focused on here in the Realm was to create a Magic Formula to defeat the Evil Sorcerer. Apparently, a Magician had gone rogue and figured out a way to horde all the Magic in the Realm for himself. He thwarted the other Magicians and sabotaged them whenever he could.

"No one knows his real identity," the Master Magician informed me. "That's because he's shrouded himself in secrecy. Every time we think we've found him, he disappears again."

"How does he disappear?" I asked.

"He moves in the shadows," she replied. "His presence overshadows everyone in this Realm, but no one has actually laid eyes on him. We don't know his real name. We simply refer to him as the Evil Sorcerer."

I asked her, "How can I help?"

She replied, "The mission in this Realm is to decipher the Magic Formula of Success that will defeat the Evil Sorcerer once and for all. Should you fail in your mission, you'll be exploded into oblivion, along with the rest of the Magicians in the Realm who fail."

Then she waved her Magic wand, blew me a kiss, and declared me to be a Magician. She gave me a Magician hat and told me to put it on. I was confused, so I asked, "Just like that?"

She responded, "Just like that. Now, go do some Magic."

Naturally, I put on my Magician hat and promptly followed her instructions. Had I been in my right mind, I might have asked myself, *What's the worst-case scenario?* But that question, unfortunately, went unasked and unanswered until it actually occurred.

The first thing I did was to start building my team. I found myself a Magic Coder who seemed to me, at the time, to be the smartest of all the Magicians in the Realm. I found him by typing a command into one of the Magic tablets that everyone else was using. We didn't meet face-to-face until many years after our relationship began, which was very odd in hindsight. But that wasn't the only strange thing about how our relationship started. The biggest oddity is that we had zero discussion in the beginning of our relationship about whether we shared the same ethics and values. Maybe that's why things went so wrong later in the relationship. We had different values all along, which I failed to recognize until it was too late.

In any case, we signed a deal together where he would create the Magic and I would sell it. We would use the income from our business to fund our research and eventually decipher the Magic Formula of Success. We would then share that formula with our fellow Magicians, and together, we would defeat the Evil Sorcerer.

That was our plan, and that's how our story began.

> Our arrangement worked, until it didn't. We tried and tried until we couldn't. Then we fought and fought until we shouldn't. He didn't do what I told him to, and I didn't know what to do.

> The reason I picked him was because his work seemed exceptional. The reason he picked me was because I let him work on his own schedule. Things fell apart when I realized his work was not so exceptional and when I asked him to work on my schedule.

But wait, there's more!

> Not enough people bought the Magic we were selling, and we didn't know what the hell kind of story we were telling. Our timing was bad and our story was sad. The Magic exploded and we imploded. We went our separate ways.

From that experience I learned that I must be wise at every turn in order not to burn. I learned to stop pretending, control my spending, and not worry about blending.

I learned it's smart to build a team, as long as it's the A-Team. People who don't fit together should split altogether. The longer they wait to separate, the more their hate will escalate.

I also learned the market has a place for me, but only if I pick the right market for me. I must find my target, and mark it, and learn better how to market.

After that experience, I wanted to take off my Magician hat and become an Explorer once again. But I didn't know how to do that without upsetting the Master Magician.

I was too shy to go back to her, afraid of what she might say. I certainly didn't want to be exploded into oblivion. So I went back to the boy who brought me here and asked whether he could help. Perhaps he could show me how to disappear and then reappear as an Explorer instead of a Magician.

The boy laughed in my face and chided me, "Trying to break the rules, are you? Tsk, tsk, tsk. I should report you to Mama."

"Please don't," I begged him. "How about we just keep this between us?"

"No."

"Please."

"No way."

"Pretty please."

He sighed. I sighed. Then he said, "Fine. Okay. But here's the deal. If you can't create the Magic Formula, you need to at least help us create it. Maybe you can explore our Realm and help us 'find our Treasure' the way you explored the Blue Ocean and found your Treasure. Same concept, different environment. Just imagine our Magic Formula is like a hidden Treasure and your mission is to find it. What do you say?"

I thought about it for a minute, and it seemed like a reasonable request. So I agreed. Then the boy shared with me his theory. He had a gut instinct that the Magic Formula of Success was hidden in plain sight in one or more of the many secret laboratories of the Realm.

"The problem as I see it," said the boy, "is that the Magicians guard their secrets fanatically. There's no way of telling whether someone has already stumbled on the Formula without realizing it. Maybe an Explorer like you can help us by bringing a new and different perspective to our work. Why don't you do some exploring, learn our ways, and see how you can help?"

But I voiced a concern: "I don't see how I could help because the Magicians will look at my Magician hat and think I'm a Magician like them. They won't open up to me because they won't see me as an Explorer. That's why I need your help. Please help me disappear and then reappear as an Explorer."

The boy looked at me as though I said something really stupid, and then he said, "Dude. I can't hold your hand forever. Stop asking for permission. Just do it."

"But how? How can I disappear and reappear?"

"It's called Reinventing Yourself. Simply take off your Magician hat, pull out your Explorer passport, and start exploring. You have the Magician hat and Warrior glasses in case you need them. Use them whenever you must. But whatever you do, *stop* asking permission to change Roles."

"It's that simple?"

"It's that simple."

I was offended by the boy's tone and directive, but I realized he might have a point. I did have a tendency to trap myself in Roles that I eventually outgrew—both in my Life and in my Business. I made a mental note to give myself permission to change Roles moving forward.

I figured this simple decision would help me to stop feeling trapped when in Reality, I wasn't trapped at all. After all, I thought, *Why should I wait for someone else to give me freedom when I was perfectly capable of freeing myself?*

So just like that, I bid the boy goodbye, took off my Magician hat, and pulled out my Explorer passport. Then I went on a little excursion. I began to knock on doors and ask the Magicians to define for me their meaning of Success.

I thought to myself, *If I could learn their definition of Success, I may be able to decipher the Magic Formula for them.* I asked them directly by saying, "I'd like to help you find the Formula, but I can't find it unless I know what it looks like. Could you help me understand what Success looks like to you?"

I heard a myriad of answers that had some common themes. From what I could gather, here's the definition of Success, according to the Magicians:

> Success means having the freedom to spend all day creating Magic. Not having that freedom would be tragic.

> Success means creativity. We seek no other activity.

> Success means knowing the details, so we can blaze our own trails.

> Success means laughing and playing around the clock, not frowning and drowning in gridlock.

> Success means making dreams come true for people who don't have a clue.

> Success means making a difference, not wasting our days in indifference.

> Success means creating efficient systems and freeing up time. Solving complex problems is our pastime.

> Success means finding hidden insights and uncovering clues with our Magic flashlights.

Success means not being manipulated, so we can avoid getting frustrated.

We fear getting tricked by things we can't predict.

And then it clicked!

I figured it out. If I could somehow free up their time to create their own Magic, the Magicians were smart enough to figure out the Magic Formula themselves. I just needed to find a way to give them the space they needed to do their thing.

The Evil Sorcerer was distracting them, so I needed to distract the Evil Sorcerer. I thought to myself, *If I could get the Evil Sorcerer off their backs, the Magicians could get back to work and achieve their definition of Success.*

So that's what I did. Sort of. I started outlining a plan, a step-by-step system, to draw out the Evil Sorcerer from the shadows. The first thing I did was to ask the Magicians to break down for me what their day looks like. I gave them pen and paper—you know, those old relics from the past. Then I asked them to set their timers to go off every thirty minutes.

"Whenever the timer goes off," I instructed them, "write down on the piece of paper everything you did in the past thirty minutes. Then repeat this every thirty minutes throughout the day. After doing this for one week, turn in your papers and we'll highlight the parts of your day where the Evil Sorcerer interrupted you. In this way, we can find the Evil Sorcerer in the details of how he moves throughout your day and distracts you.

"Any time you spend not creating Magic is time the Evil Sorcerer is stealing from you. We can't get that time back, unless we know the specific details of how he's stealing it from you. Once we discover those details, we'll decipher your specific Magic Formula of Success! We'll isolate the Evil Sorcerer and bring him into the light of day. Then we'll banish him from the Realm."

They looked at me skeptically but agreed to follow my lead. For one day only. They said, "We'll give you twenty-four hours."

I insisted, "I need a week."

They countered, "Three days."

I agreed.

After three days, the Magicians turned in their papers, and I examined them. I isolated the times when the Evil Sorcerer interrupted their days, and I highlighted those sections. I discovered a pattern.

I gathered the Magicians and shared with them my findings. They were amazed. Enthralled. Ecstatic. They called *me* a Magician. I had earned their trust by delving into the details of their challenging puzzle and then giving them a step-by-step plan for how to solve it.

We uncovered the hidden identity of the Evil Sorcerer and discovered his real name was Mr. Interruption. Mr. Interruption would interrupt the Magicians at all times of their day, distracting them from creating Magic. He would manipulate them with addictive technologies called Social Media, Apps, and News Feeds. These shiny objects were expertly crafted with built-in Notifications and Gamification.

Mr. Interruption preyed on the Magicians' FOMO (fear of missing out) and did everything in his power to increase their engagement with his many platforms. He used that "engagement" to serve them ads on a platter from which he made billions, if not trillions, in wealth for himself. In this manner, he accumulated and then hoarded all the wealth in the Realm.

More importantly, Mr. Interruption frustrated the Magicians and tricked them into doing things that they didn't want to do, distracting them from creating their Magic. But wait, there's more!

Mr. Interruption also had an assistant called Do-It-Yourself. Do-It-Yourself would assign to the Magicians work that could easily, and for a much lower cost, be delegated to others. Do-It-Yourself (DIY) was a nasty creature who had sharp talons that dug deep into the Magicians' brains. His grip was firm as he whispered into their ears that they were the only ones capable of doing work that should be delegated. He would trap them, hold them hostage, and distract them from creating the Magic they were born to create.

We dragged Mr. Interruption and his nasty assistant, Do-It-Yourself, through the streets of the Realm. We deposited them at the feet of the Master Magician and shared with her our findings. We told her all about their deceptions, their trickery, and their devious ways. We asked her to pass her sentence and decide the fate of these obnoxious creatures.

The Master Magician decided that instead of banishing Mr. Interruption and Do-It-Yourself from the Realm, she would isolate them into a corner for the rest of their days. In this manner, they could watch from the sidelines of insignificance while the Magicians created their Magic. *That* would be their punishment.

And so it came to pass that Mr. Interruption was allowed to visit the Magicians no more than twice per day, but never on a Friday. Or a Saturday. Or a Sunday.

The twice-daily visits, four days per week, would be scheduled consistently each day, and the Magicians themselves would pick the times that worked best for them.

As for Do-It-Yourself, we created two algorithms to box him into a corner.

MAGIC FORMULA #1 FOR COMMISSION-BASED SALESPERSONS AND ENTREPRENEURS

We asked each Magician who was a business owner or commission-based salesperson to calculate their hourly rate of pay. Then we asked them to delegate to others any work that could be performed for less than the Magician's hourly rate of pay. Here's the Magic Formula:

Current or Desired Annual Income   Number of Hours Worked per Year = Hourly Rate of Pay. For example, a person who works forty hours per week for fifty weeks per year works a total of 2,000 hours per year. If that person earns or should be earning $200,000 per year, their hourly rate would be $100 per hour ($200,000 2,000 hours = $100 per hour). If a task can be performed for significantly less than that, it would be snatched away from the clutches of Do-It-Yourself and delegated to someone else at the appropriate rate of pay.

If a salesperson or an entrepreneur started feeling over-whelmed or burned out, they would take out their pen and paper. Then they'd keep track of their activities for three days and run their Magic Formula. In this manner, the Magicians could continually promote themselves and free themselves from Roles they had outgrown. Their Coaches and Leaders would be responsible for keeping them on track.

MAGIC FORMULA #2 FOR OPERATIONS STAFF AND SALARIED BUSINESS PROFESSIONALS

We asked each salaried Magician to create a list of work activities that they were uniquely qualified to perform and that gave them the most joy. We asked them to define the specific value those activities create for the team and for the clients served by the team.

Then we asked the Magicians to create a second list of work activities they were doing that seemed to drain their energy. We asked them to define the specific value those activities create for the team and for the clients served by the team.

Finally, we asked the Magicians to reallocate their work activities so that each Magician could remain focused on the activities that (a) were tailored to their unique skill-sets, (b) gave them the most joy, and (c) created the most value for the team and the clients served by the team.

For tasks that nobody at all wanted, we would examine the root cause of why that task exists. Then we would create or purchase Magic Technology to make that task go away.

If a salaried Magician started feeling overwhelmed or burned out, they would take out their pen and paper. Then they'd keep track of their activities for three days and run their Magic Formula. In this manner, the Magicians could continually promote themselves and free themselves from Roles they had outgrown. Their Coaches and Leaders would be responsible for keeping them on track.

From here on in, Mr. Interruption and Do-It-Yourself would be relegated to the sidelines while the Magicians made their Magic. The Magicians got back control of their time and unlocked their Magic Formula of Success. Some Magicians became Masters of Sales and Entrepreneurs. When their workload got to be too much, they used their Magic Formula, broke free from the Roles they had trapped themselves in, and promoted themselves. They invested in themselves, paid for their own assistants, and didn't ask anybody for handouts. They took control of their destiny, achieving their definition of Success.

Some Magicians became Masters of Operations and Leaders. They used their Magic Formula to help others succeed. They forced Mr. Interruption back into his little corner. They freed up Time, solved complex problems, and created efficient systems. They made dreams come true with their Magic. They did this in laboratories of Finance, Housing, Technology, and all other labs of the Realm. Many even applied their Magic Formula in the laboratory of Government and Politics, shedding themselves of outdated Roles.

In this manner, the Magicians found Meaning and Joy in their work, which was their definition of Success. The same giggling girls I had met on the Isle of Explorers had somehow managed to sneak into this Realm as well. "Hello, my friend!" They greeted me cheerfully as they took my hands and began to dance. Together we danced the night away, along with some of my fellow Magicians.

Some Magicians, however, refused to dance with us. They spat in the faces of Meaning and Joy as they squandered their opportunity to do meaningful work and create unique value for others. Instead, they became Incompetent Fools. They made Life and Business difficult for others in the Realm due to their sloppiness and apathy. They blamed others for their failures, created completely avoidable "bugs," recklessly dropped "balls," and arrogantly created "WTF" moments whenever they could.

I later figured out a way for my fellow Magicians and me to minimize our exposure to those Incompetent Fools. But that's another story for another time. As for this story, it was party time!

After the Magicians and I defeated the Evil Sorcerer, we met up with the other children in the candy store to celebrate our victory. The group of children who had first accompanied me to this Realm had somehow managed to learn how to appear and disappear using various Magic Formulas they created in the Tunnel of Technology.

The timid boy and girl whom I first met on my voyage into this Realm were not so timid any longer. They too had apparently found Meaning and Joy. They giggled infectiously as they sang to me the songs of their heart, which had been buried in silence for too long.

Some of the other children who accompanied us into this Realm created new identities for themselves and decided to become Magicians. Others decided to go back to the Isle of Explorers, whereas others decided it was time for them to visit the other Realms. We all found common ground because we became honorary members of the Society of Magicians. The boy who brought us to this Realm rewarded us for our efforts with honorary membership.

He then treated us to bowls of sugary candy, boxes of delicious chocolates, and buckets of gelato and ice cream in the candy store. I was personally most enthralled with the magic gummy bears (hint, hint), although I had to limit my intake of them so as not to get sick. They were only legal in certain parts of the Realm, and I made sure not to break any laws as I partook. The chocolate hazelnut gelato made for the most deliciously refreshing after-gummy snack. Now, in hindsight, I think I may have had too much.

As we swapped stories and Magic tricks, the boy asked me what lessons I had learned in this Realm. I told him how I had learned that Magicians want to create Magic—for themselves and others. They want to be creative, and they are keenly interested in the details of how Magic is performed. I explained how I earned their trust by unveiling the mysteries that troubled them and by enabling them to create Magic in the way they wanted.

The boy nodded in approval and told me The Chairman would be proud. I raised my eyebrows and was about to ask how he knew The Chairman.

But before I could ask, we were interrupted by loud music that some child decided to turn on. It wasn't the kind of music I expected.

Frank Sinatra started crooning in his classic manner over the speakers, along with his Rat Pack. The children and I began to dance the night away until the summer wind came blowing in from across the sea. It lingered there, touched her hair, and then stopped.

I realized I was dancing with my Worthy Rival, who had popped into this very same establishment unbeknownst to me.

I wondered how *she* got here and I quickly let go of her hand when I realized it was *her* that I was dancing with.

She winked at me seductively with a come-hither look, and then a naughty grin formed across her lips. She leaned in and whispered in my ear, "Guess what, Buttercup? While you've been building one relationship at a time, I've figured out another Magic Formula called Enterprise Sales."

"Interesting. Tell me more."

"I've got a better idea. How about I *show* you?" Then she turned and walked away, knowing my eyes would follow her, and then my body. Which they did.

She lured me into the back of the candy store, where it seemed as if she was going to show me some extra special treats. I followed her, wondering what kind of delicacies she had in store for me. Then suddenly, I lost my bearings and completely blacked out.

When I awoke, I found myself in a frigid, dungeon-like place, where the tension was so thick you could cut through the air. Then I felt it, a razor-sharp knife flying across my face, cutting me, trying to hack me to pieces.

Little did I know that my Worthy Rival had transported me into the Kingdom of Rulers, where I would soon lose all my Magic. I would later find out that she had led me straight into the Dungeon of Corporate Politics.

There, I would be required to undergo sadistic hazing rituals and provide satisfactory answers to the list of Endless Questions.

I had no warning of how the Pantheon of Pride would change me into someone I barely recognized and trap me in a prison from which I would barely escape.

I had no clue that the gods of Legal Compliance, the gods of Change and Competition, and the gods of Economic Uncertainty would nearly exterminate me with their bolts of lightning.

If only someone had warned me about not chasing after my Worthy Rival. Or maybe someone did. I only wish now that I had heeded the warning.

CHAPTER 5

The Kingdom
of Rulers

THE MISSION:

Help us tame the Chaos in our kingdom before
your Contract runs out...or we'll banish you forever.

I FOUND MYSELF IN THE COURT OF RULERS COURTING RULERS
of all types:

> I saw Rulers with big, bad hair, and others with balding
> heads and no hair. I saw Black Rulers who gave inspira-
> tional orations and White Rulers bloodied by bush-league
> and pro-league confrontations.

> I saw Rulers who inherited conflicts they didn't ask for, and
> others who were plunged into battles they were expected
> to not fight. I saw Rulers who were judged for not creating
> Magic after being stripped of their ability to create Magic.
> Then I saw Rulers who were expected to grant passports of
> freedom to people who confiscated the freedom of others.

> I saw brave Rulers who shattered glass ceilings, paving the
> way for those who came after them. Then I saw weak Rulers
> who bumped into imaginary ceilings while creating ceilings
> of steel for others to bump into.

> I saw Evil Rulers who stripped people of their human iden-
> tity and then blamed them for walking around without
> identification. I saw greedy Rulers who plundered the Trea-
> sures of foreign cultures and then told cultured foreigners
> they were most unwelcome to share in those Treasures.

> Then I saw Good Rulers who did Good in spite of Evil, and
> Wise Rulers who were generous despite the greed of others.
> The Good and Wise Rulers strived to be as good and wise as
> Solomon, forgetting that Solomon himself was neither good
> enough nor wise enough to keep one woman happy.

But wait, let me back up a minute. I forgot to tell you how I got to the Court of Rulers in the first place. My admittance was either pure luck or sheer madness. I'm still trying to figure that one out.

After my Worthy Rival seduced me into the Dungeon of Corporate Politics, I was almost hacked to pieces by sharp razors hurled at me from all directions. I later found out that Rulers require newcomers in their Realm to go through a hazing ritual called Death by a Thousand Meetings.

The ritual is quite simple: Throw as many meetings as you can at the new person to see whether they can survive with their sanity intact. If the new person gets hacked to pieces, no one will know. The new person will simply disappear, never to bother you or anyone else ever again. But if the new person survives the hazing ritual, they are taken in chains from the Dungeon of Corporate Politics and escorted to the Court of Rulers.

In the Court of Rulers, they'll be questioned endlessly and be required to give their responses in bullet points via executive summaries not lasting more than one page. If the responses to the Endless Questions are satisfactory, their chains will be removed. But wait, there's more!

If you're lucky enough to make it past the Death by a Thousand Meetings hazing ritual, and if your bullet-point responses to Endless Questions are satisfactory, you'll undergo a third stage of approval. This is known as the RFP stage, which I think is short for "request for proposal" or perhaps "rest forever peacefully" for the majority who don't make it past this stage.

During the RFP phase, you'll be lined up with your competitors and then stripped down as though you work in a brothel. The one most suitable to the onlooker is then chosen. The rest are invited to "rest forever peacefully."

As far as the one chosen by the onlooker, it's most definitely a subjective process (wink, wink). Some are chosen because of their looks, others because of their gender, and others because of their majority or minority status.

Some are chosen because they are obnoxious and loud, and others simply because they can please a crowd. Very few are chosen because of the quality of their work or for the simple fact that they are most suitable for the position.

By some twist of fate, I made it past the hazing ritual in the Dungeon of Corporate Politics with no more than a few scratches. I also managed to provide satisfactory answers to the list of Endless Questions. I even survived the RFP stage, though I had no idea why. This placed me in the fourth and final stage of orientation, called Contract Negotiation.

During this stage of my orientation, I was required to undergo a series of steps called due diligence and legal review. This included, but was not limited to, absolving the Rulers of all responsibility for anything and everything. Meanwhile, I was expected to take personal responsibility for anything and everything.

I'm not sure why they called it a negotiation, as nothing was up for negotiation. The Rulers got what they wanted, and I had to pretend that I also got what I wanted in order to move forward.

I passed this final stage of orientation and was admitted into the Kingdom of Rulers.

They took away my passport of free travel and gave me a Contract instead. They also told me to put away my Warrior glasses and my Magician hat because I would not be allowed to use them in this Realm.

It was against their policy for me to fight back against them as a Warrior or perform any Magic at all in the Realm. I must adhere strictly to the terms of my Contract, which stated that I would be free to travel within this Realm for a designated period of time—if I followed the Rules and if the Rulers didn't get bored with me.

If they did get bored with me, they'd simply withhold my payments or make my life difficult, knowing that it would be more costly for me to take them to court than for me to simply walk away.

After my Contract expires, I may be lucky enough to be invited to apply for a Contract Renewal. In that case, I would need to repeat the entire orientation process, including the Death by a Thousand Meetings hazing ritual, the phase of Endless Questions, followed by the RFP phase, followed by another round of Contract Negotiations. This process would repeat itself on an annual basis, into perpetuity, or for the rest of my time here in the Realm.

"Sounds like a real treat," I told the Rulers at my Contract signing. As I signed my life away, I wondered where my Worthy Rival was and what she was doing. I wondered whether she had orchestrated this "treat" for me instead of the luscious delicacies that I had been expecting her to show me when I followed after her in the candy store. She had completely disappeared after depositing me into the Dungeon of Corporate Politics, and I wondered if I'd ever hear from her again.

After my Contract signing, I met the Ice Queen and the Bombastic Boss who ruled the Realm with iron fists and rigid rules. She ate delicacies of the most exotic nature, and he ate gluttonously, with an insatiable appetite for just about everything. Together, they made the perfect pairing.

As for the Realm itself, there was a grill in every capital, and I dined in them all. The Capitalists rubbed their ribeyes with porcini mushrooms and glazed their steaks with balsamic. They filled their mac and cheese with lobster. Lots of lobster. From Maine. I ate towers of seafood and buckets of truffle fries.

I was a Ruler among Rulers, and I ate like a king. I acquired a taste for fine wine with dinner, followed by port wine after dinner. For a nightcap, I was introduced to French Armagnac, which I liked better than French cognac.

My belly grew a few sizes, and I started to wear jeans with a suit jacket instead of a custom-tailored suit. I figured this was the next natural progression as my wardrobe evolved toward the athletic jumpsuits worn by The Chairman.

But I wasn't ready to give up my suit jacket just yet. It seemed to hide my growing belly. I feared an athletic jumpsuit would simply accentuate it.

Just as I was getting comfortable with my place in the Realm, I was admitted into the Pantheon of Pride, where I took my rightful place among the most distinguished Rulers in the kingdom. The Pantheon was the seat of power, and it was located in the Cloud, on top of the highest mountain in the Realm.

It was supported by massive Columns of Data that the Rulers had built to document how great they were. There were Demos and Displays where Rulers showcased their magnificence for everyone to see. I saw Leaderboards and Follower Counts where they measured their popularity. I saw Mirrored Statues that the Rulers would gaze into, worshipping themselves.

I couldn't help but marvel at the magnificence of the Pantheon and the Titans who worshipped each other here. Then I was awestruck with a sense of my own significance, having made it here from such humble beginnings. Just as I was worshipping the Mirrored Statue of myself, climaxing in my own Pride, I heard a rumbling sound and the ground beneath me began to shake.

Then quite suddenly, and without my permission, my Mirrored Statue collapsed before me and I was nearly struck by a bolt of lightning. The gods of Legal Compliance, the gods of Change and Competition, and the gods of Economic Uncertainty came riding into the Pantheon on their Chariots of Authority.

The chariots dripped with blood and were drawn by dreadful flying dragons cloaked in pure white, as if to disguise their hideous nature. The gods flung bolts of lightning, aiming them at the Rulers as though they were intruders in this great Pantheon of Pride. The dragons fueled the fires created by the lightning, wreaking destruction everywhere.

The Rulers, who had just a moment ago seemed to me like gods themselves, began to flee and disperse as though they were cowards. They retreated into the corners of the Pantheon, underneath their own crumbled Mirrored Statues, hoping to save themselves from the bolts of lightning being hurled at them.

After the lightning storm, and the baptism of fire that followed it, the Pantheon of Pride was littered with Chaos. The Chaos was like a black organism that grew from the wreckage with each passing second. It grew so monstrous that it split into two organisms.

In this manner, by growing monstrous and splitting off, the Chaos would multiply until it covered everything in its wake. It would drip from the Pantheon across the entire Realm, baptizing the people with a constant shower of Chaos.

As the Chaos began to grow and multiply out of the wreckage of the lightning and dragon fire, the gods of Legal Compliance, the gods of Change and Competition, and the gods of Economic Uncertainty gathered the Rulers into the middle of the Pantheon. Apparently, there was to be a special announcement.

"Your mission," the gods announced to the Rulers, "is to tame the Chaos in the Realm that we have created for you. Once you tame the Chaos, we will invade again and shower you with even more Chaos. If you survive the first round of Chaos, we will allow you to apply for a Contract Renewal to see if you're eligible to remain for the second round."

And just like that, after nearly destroying the Pantheon with their lightning bolts and dragon fire, and after baptizing the kingdom with their Chaos, the gods of Legal Compliance, the gods of Change and Competition, and the gods of Economic Uncertainty rode away in their Chariots of Authority.

I looked around me at the growing Chaos and decided to help the Rulers tame it. Each instance of Chaos was multiplying before our eyes. It grew and reproduced itself to the tune of a Ticking Clock, which the gods had left in the Pantheon to watch over the Rulers.

The Ticking Clock had two hands and one all-seeing Eye. It would tick-tick-tick with each passing second, reminding the Rulers that their minutes, hours, and days were numbered.

The Ticking Clock made random announcements through-out each day as religiously as a minaret's call to prayer. It pronounced with precision how the gods of Legal Compliance, the gods of Change and Competition, and the gods of Economic Uncertainty would return at some point in Time of their own choosing.

These constant random announcements terrified the Rulers, making the wise ones among them continuously vigilant, even during the minutes, hours, and days when the Chaos seemed to be tame.

In witnessing all this, I couldn't help but marvel at the irony. I realized that even Rulers have Rulers, and the Ticking Clock rules them all. I began to empathize with the Rulers and their unfortunate situation. I tried to think of creative ways to help them tame the Chaos invading their Realm.

The best way I knew how to be creative was to play a little trick on myself. I pretended to put aside my Ruler Contract and imagined myself wearing my confiscated Magician hat.

I imagined doing this even though I had no permission to do so. I figured they can take away most things from me in this Realm, but the one thing they'll never be able to take away is my own mind. My own imagination. I don't need anybody's permission to think. So I did think. Even though thinking is underrated. And often frowned upon.

By thinking like a Magician, I thought of an idea that only a Magician would think of. *What if we could shovel the Chaos into various boxes or compartments and then seal the Chaos inside? In this manner, we could limit the impact of the Chaos in the same way we the Magicians limited the impact of Mr. Interruption.*

But then I thought about it some more and realized that wouldn't be enough. Like any toxic substance that grows with each passing second, The Chaos would eventually break out of the sealed compartments and overflow into the Realm. So I took off my imaginary Magician hat and pretended to put on my confiscated Warrior glasses. Then I thought of an idea that only a Warrior would think of.

We could, at a time of our own choosing, pick our own battle and launch a surprise attack on the Chaos. We could unseal the boxes and hack away at the Chaos like a Warrior hacks away at an Enemy. With disciplined precision. With targeted focus. With unrelenting drive. In this manner, we would rule over the Chaos instead of allowing the Chaos to rule over us.

Some instances of the Chaos we could completely destroy by hacking away until we found and eliminated the root cause. Other instances of the Chaos we could simply tame by compartmentalizing it and hacking away at it only during certain periods of the day. This would be similar to the way the Master Magician had sentenced Mr. Interruption to his twice-daily visits.

In this manner, we could create a Paradise of Peace in this Realm of Reality, in spite of the Chaos that would never be fully eliminated. I put together a short executive summary with simple bullet points:

1. Shovel the Chaos into boxes.

2. Seal the boxes of Chaos.

3. Unseal the boxes of Chaos at a time of our own choosing, but before the Chaos breaks out.

4. Attack the Chaos with skill and precision.

5. Uncover the root cause of the Chaos and eliminate it.

6. When the root cause of the Chaos can't be eliminated:

   a. Tame the Chaos as best as possible in the manner described above.

   b. Disclose truthfully to the people in the Realm the root cause of the Chaos and the reason it must be tamed instead of eliminated.

I ran my executive summary by my fellow Rulers. I shared my ideas in as simple and concise a manner as I knew how. Some of them laughed in my face. They said I was completely unqualified to give them advice, and they weren't interested in my help.

But I did find a few who were willing to give my idea a try. Those few became my Clients, and I began to serve them as best I could. I helped them to tame the Chaos in their areas of the Realm.

Without even realizing it, I no longer saw myself as a Ruler in the Realm, but as a servant of the Realm. My primary mission was to help the Rulers tame the Chaos. My secondary mission, however, was to help them enjoy Life in the Realm as best as they could in spite of the Chaos. Together, we'd create our own Paradise of Peace despite the Chaos that would never go away.

That's how I found myself in the Court of Rulers courting Rulers of all types. I found Rulers who were interested in splitting tomahawk steaks with me at expensive restaurants. My proposal to them was quite simple: "Why eat a small steak alone when we could split a large steak together?"

Many of them agreed, especially the ones who ate their meat medium rare like me. Some took a picture of me gnawing on the bone afterward, as my otherwise classy grandmother used to do after eating her steaks.

The Rulers told me of their experiences on their Journey, and I told them of my experiences on mine. I discovered that many Rulers had started out their Journey as I did, in the Arena of Warriors. We swapped stories of The Chairman and of our many battles with our Worthy Rivals. We drank lots of fine wine together while remembering the delicious burgers we once ate at the Winner's Club back when Life was simpler.

One day, a Global Pandemic flew overhead, spreading a nasty virus across the Realm. It caused most of us to stay locked up in our homes for many days and nights. During one such day and night, I found myself dining alone with my favorite bottle of wine.

My Beloved Memories decided to pay me a visit, and I poured them a glass. Together, we sipped our wine and spoke of days gone by. I told my Beloved Memories about the lessons I had learned in this Kingdom of Rulers. I told them about the Chaos and how although it could be tamed, it would never completely go away.

I told them how Rulers need to be communicated with in bullet points and short executive summaries. That's because they're super busy taming the Chaos in the Realm. They need quick, practical solutions to complex problems.

I explained how even Rulers have Rulers, and the Ticking Clock rules them all. I shared how the best way to navigate this Realm is to see yourself as a servant, not as a Ruler. Then you may serve the Realm by serving the people in the Realm.

I advised them that the primary mission is to help the people in the Realm tame the Chaos. The secondary mission is to help the people in the Realm enjoy Life as best as they can, knowing the Chaos will never fully go away.

My Beloved Memories and I had many conversations in those days, over many bottles of wine. Yet, something inside me began to long for simpler times and the camaraderie I once felt with my fellow StorySellers when I initially set out on my Journey. I started drinking more and more until I needed many more drinks.

I was ready to leave this Realm. I began to count the days until my Contract ran out. I would not seek to renew it.

When my Contract finally did run out, I was handed back my Explorer passport, my Warrior glasses, and my Magician hat. To me, though, they were more or less symbols at that point. I was ready to embark on the next phase of my Journey, with or without the symbols.

But first, another drink. And then another. And then another. In a drunken stupor, I somehow managed to escape the Kingdom of Rulers one evening. I stumbled into a Club where there was even more alcohol. Lots and lots of alcohol. And peanuts. Lots and lots of peanuts.

Little did I know that I had stumbled into the Club of Comedians, where I would learn to laugh again. And eat lots of peanuts. I had no clue that my Worthy Rival would enter the picture and steal (again) what was rightfully mine.

Nor did I have any idea that I'd meet a king who dressed like a tiger and looked like a tiger. Or that I would be mesmerized by a gorgeous beauty who resembled a pied piper.

I had no clue that I'd meet the Boring One and how utterly uncool he'd be (compared to me).

I only wish that I had been more sober as I stumbled into that Club, because the exact details of what happened next would have been worth remembering. But we'll need to content ourselves with the crazy story as it was told to me without censoring.

CHAPTER 6

The Club of Comedians

THE MISSION:

Make us laugh and entertain us...or we'll tell the entire world how utterly boring and uncool you are.

WHAT HAPPENED WAS...

I was looking for something to make me laugh after serving my time and a half. I spent too long in the Dungeon of Corporate Politics, so I started looking for a brand-new fix.

I almost didn't survive Death by a Thousand Meetings, and I was quite tired of taking beatings. I was done with the Endless Questions and making always-unheeded suggestions. I wasn't interested in another Contract Negotiation. I simply wanted to drink my libation.

I wanted to get happy, and I didn't want to feel crappy. I wanted to be entertained so I could get unchained from the awful Reality in which I had found myself detained.

So I had too much to drink, and I couldn't quite think. The way I should have, or how I could have. And that's how I ended up in the Comedy Club.

I saw Comedians who were hilarious, and others who were nefarious. I laughed at bad jokes and started making dad jokes. They nearly kicked me out, but then I began to shout. I yelled and screamed so loud that it really startled the crowd. They couldn't figure out how to handle me, so they began to manhandle me. I heckled the announcer and got rough with the bouncer. I got turned about and then I blacked out.

After the unfortunate incident, I wallowed in shame. I had a bad headache and started passing blame. I didn't want to get bitter or be a transmitter of negative energy via vibes and twitter. I just wanted to laugh and have fun after my hard-fought run.

After I sobered up, I knocked on the door of the Comedy Club, hoping they'd let me in again. I was greeted by a king who dressed like a tiger and looked like a tiger. He was a nasty fellow and his clothes were all yellow. He invited me in to take a look at the show he was about to cook.

He gave me quite a fright but didn't recognize me from last night. So I thought, What could go wrong? And boy, was I wrong!

The people in the Club thought he was super funny, but to me his show was a waste of money.

I walked out and went to another Club. And then I saw *her*.

My Worthy Rival was in the other Club entertaining the good old boys and trying to catch what she referred to as a "big one." I stared at her as she moved about, whispering god-knows-what in the ears of all the people.

I couldn't do what she could do because I didn't have what she clearly has. She has a way of getting about—I'll give her that much.

They laughed and giggled as she tickled their fancy. I couldn't understand why, and I started getting antsy. She gave me a quick glance, and I looked away. I couldn't bear to see her this way.

She was the center of attention. Even I was paying attention. I couldn't peel my gaze away, and then she started coming my way. She leaned in with a wiggle and whispered something that made me giggle. I can't even remember what she said, maybe something about a bed?

I asked her what she was doing and then she started cooing. She asked me if I could be funny, so I tried to say something funny. She didn't laugh at my apparent gaffe. Instead, she turned to the crowd as if she'd won, pointed her finger at me, and yelled, "He's the Boring One!"

The crowd went wild. They rushed at me and went to kick me out of this Club just like I was kicked out of the other one the night before. Only this time, I was completely sober and tried to think the way I should have and as best as I could have.

"Wait!" I begged the crowd. "Hang on a sec. Is there anything I can do to stick around? I just wanted to catch a few laughs. I didn't mean to be offensive to anyone."

The crowd looked at me funny, and the announcer replied, "Okay, fine. You have one chance." I asked, "One chance for what?"

"One chance to make us laugh. If you can't make us laugh, we'll banish you from the Club and label you as 'The Boring One.' We don't like people who are Boring or people who are Uncool. You seem both Boring and Uncool. We'll give you one chance to prove you're not. If you fail, we'll kick you out of this Club and forever banish you from the Realm."

"That's harsh."

"That's Reality."

"Whose Reality?"

"Ours. And now, yours."

"Okay, fine."

"Fine?"

"Yes. Fine. I'll take you up on your offer. I'll give it my best shot. But first, can I please have a shot?"

He glared at me. I glared back. *First person to talk loses!* I lost.

"Okay, okay. No shots before I give it a shot. Here goes..."

I racked my brain thinking of something funny to say. I thought of knock-knock jokes and all sorts of dad jokes. But I was too afraid to pull any of them out because I didn't want to get kicked out.

I wanted to be admitted into this Club, but I knew in my heart that I just wasn't funny enough. I saw myself as a Serious Intellectual, not as a Funny Comedian. Words eluded me as fear gripped me.

Then the booing started. First a heckler in the back of the Club. Then it grew and grew until the entire crowd was booing in unison at the Boring One in front of them. They started yelling at me to get out. So I did. Sort of.

I left the Club and sat on the outside wondering how I could ever make it back in. I wanted to be entertained. But before they would entertain me, they wanted me to entertain them. It didn't make any sense. I wanted them to make *me* laugh, and they expected me to make *them* laugh. *How weird!*

Then someone walked up to me and asked, "Why so sad? You look so mad. Did you do something bad?"

I looked up and answered, "I wanted them to make me laugh, but they kicked me out and called me the Boring One. It seems so unfair."

"What's unfair?"

"They wanted me to make them laugh."

"And?"

"I wanted them to make *me* laugh."

"And?"

"What do you mean, 'And?'"

"Dude. Let me get this straight. You wanted something for nothing?"

I stared at him. He stared back. I looked away. He walked away. Then he looked back at me and said, "You people. Everyone wants something for nothing. You really *are* the Boring One. To get Value, you must give Value. Otherwise, don't be surprised if people think you have no Value."

I scratched my head in confusion, wondering what all this meant. Then *she* came out. My Worthy Rival had come out to what...admonish me? Tease me? Make fun of me? Then she said, "What's up, Buttercup?"

I looked at her funny. Then she looked at me funny. I looked away. Then she scolded me, "If you can't make them giggle and laugh, make them cry with delight—but for God's sake entertain them! Surprise them. Mesmerize them with the music of your work. Lead them to a place where they've always wanted to go and where no one has dared take them before...until now...until you."

I stammered, searching for a clever response. Then she snapped, "Stop trying to be clever. Stop being boring. Just be human. Don't you see this is hard work? You think everyone but you has it easy? The people in this Realm have it hard, just like you. Don't expect them to give you something for nothing."

Then she walked away. I saw her enter another Club, and then another. Each time she walked away with more and more followers. So I followed her too. I wondered where she was going. After visiting five Clubs with her, I saw a little girl with braided hair and a cute dress run up to her and hand her a small flute.

Then my Worthy Rival touched the flute to her lips and began playing the most beautiful melody I had ever heard. The music overwhelmed me, and I lost my bearings. When I found them again, I noticed that the entire Realm was dancing to the tune of her song. In an instant, while I stumbled around in my own Arrogance, my Worthy Rival had connected with my audience and mesmerized them.

They followed her like children following the pied piper. She led them to a place where they've always wanted to go and where no one had dared take them before. I envied her and wondered how I could ever do what she had just done.

I thought about what she said. *Don't expect them to give you something for nothing.* Then I questioned myself, *What can I give them if I'm not funny? I'm not a Comedian, like her. I'm not a musician, like her. I'm not an entertainer, like her. I'm more or less a serious person, often too serious. Does that mean I'm stuck forever in this Role as the "Boring One"?*

I tried to remember the lessons I had learned in my Journey so far. One lesson in particular stuck out. It was a lesson I had learned in the Society of Magicians when I vowed to stop asking permission to change Roles. I decided at that time to liberate myself from outdated Roles whenever I felt trapped.

Now I felt trapped in the Role of being the Boring One because I simply wasn't a funny guy. My sense of humor wasn't what *normal* people wanted. What else, besides what my Worthy Rival was doing, could I offer these people? How could I free myself of the Role of being the Boring One?

Then I remembered something else my Worthy Rival had said. *Surprise them. Mesmerize them with the music of your work. Lead them to a place where they've always wanted to go and where no one has dared take them before...until now...until you.*

Then it hit me. I could entertain others the way I entertained myself. I enjoy putting together what I believe to be clever wordplay. I often amuse myself and laugh at my own jokes. My favorite jokes are when I make fun of myself. I'm such an easy target for my kind of jokes.

I also get a kick out of insulting the Exhibitionists: the nasty, obnoxious people in the Realms of Reality who bully everyone and smack people with their shit-filled Stories. No one forced them to be that way, and they can choose to change at any time and go a different way.

I can't be the only one who's encountered Exhibitionists in their personal and professional Journey. And I really believe that not enough people stand up to them, myself included. Maybe because we don't know how to do so without getting dirty and becoming like them.

I thought to myself, *Exhibitionists are absolutely fair play for insults and wordplay! What if I could share my wordplay and insult the Exhibitionists in one of the Comedy Clubs? Would that be enough to earn me a place in this Realm?*

I figured the worst that could happen if I try is that I'll be in exactly the same position I am now. The best-case scenario if I try is that I stop being the Boring One, even if only to myself or perhaps a few others. So I moved forward with my crazy idea and displayed my work in a galleria.

I visited a Club called the Author and Podcaster Club. I created a podcast and book of wordplay to entertain and educate myself. If nobody liked my work, at least I would have had a few laughs myself and learned a few things along the way. I was afraid to share my work with others because I thought they may think I was weird or that my work was worthless.

But in spite of my fears, I decided to just pour myself a drink and go for it. I've found that my work can best be digested when paired with your favorite bottle of wine or whiskey. And peanuts. Lots and lots of peanuts. If you don't drink wine or whiskey, perhaps try chocolate and coffee. Lots and lots of coffee. If you don't drink coffee, I'm not sure how I can help you. Maybe try coconut water?

By some miraculous twist of fate, and armed with buckets of peanuts, I found enough courage to grab a platform in the Club of Comedians. I got up on my platform and did my thing. Except I wasn't a Comedian at all. I was simply a StorySeller. I shared my Story the best way I knew how, with wordplay.

This book is the result! I'm expecting it to be a turnoff to some, unusual to others, and an absolute delight to people like you and me. I'm expecting half the readers to walk out but the other half to stay. And that's okay. I'm not here for the ones who walk out. I'm here for you because you've stayed.

So tell me, are we having fun yet?

One lesson I have learned is to always make sure that my team feels entertained by their work. They need to laugh and smile just as I need to laugh and smile. Otherwise, they'll label me and the work they do with me as the Boring One. And nobody wants to be or work with the Boring One.

I also learned that my team likes to eat and drink almost as much as I do. One way to keep them laughing and smiling is to have get-togethers. And so we do. Not often enough, however.

As for my Worthy Rival, I never did meet up with her after that mesmerizing experience where she captivated me and everyone else in the Realm. But I'll always be grateful for the lessons she taught me.

That's the thing about Worthy Rivals. I've found that instead of chasing them or resenting them, it's simply best to learn from them. They're not expecting you to do that. They're expecting you to copy them or resent them or chase after them.

In my case, my Worthy Rival always pushed the boundaries and delivered an anything-but-average experience. She was kind of edgy, very trendy, and super sexy.

I'm not sure if I'd ever fit those descriptions, but I've learned how to content myself with my Clients' subscriptions. If they find value in my works, I'll keep each of my quirks. If they don't, at least I'll always have one Client: myself.

After earning a few laughs in the Club of Comedians and delighting a few people with my wordplay, I decided it was time to get something to eat. But no alcohol or peanuts this time. Maybe some water and a salad?

I wanted to think about my Unique, Authentic Winning Story. I valued the lessons I had learned in my travels through the Realms of Reality. But I still wasn't clear on what my UAWS was or should be. I needed to think clearly, but I wanted to sing and dance dearly. So I did. Sort of.

I put on some music that many would find boring, old-fashioned, and eclectic. Music like old hymns and modern pop, jazzy jazz and classic rock. Classical Arabic music followed by upbeat Latin music. Broadway musical soundtracks followed by the theme song from *Pulp Fiction*. Topped off with Neil Diamond and Etta James. Billy Joel and Aretha Franklin. Barbra Streisand and The Temptations. Tony Bennett and The Beatles. Kenny Rogers and Usher. B.B. King and John Legend. Amy Winehouse and Michael Bublé. Marvin Gaye and Louis Prima. Lionel Richie and Pitbull. Ray Charles and Elvis Presley. And, of course, Frank Sinatra. Then I danced to the tune of my own Story. Some would say that I should've stopped while I was ahead.

CHAPTER 7

The Community of Friendly Neighbors

THE MISSION:

Protect us from the Outsiders who seek to harm us...or we'll "cancel" you and treat you like an Outsider.

I DANCED MY WAY STRAIGHT INTO THE COMMUNITY OF Friendly Neighbors, where my feet moved in ways they had never moved before.

With the Latinas I danced the salsa and with the Brazilians I danced the samba. The Argentinians taught us how to tango while dancers from India served us mango.

I danced to the tune of the "Hava Nagila" with the Jews, and I danced the dabke to the beat of the derbakke with the Arabs. I danced hip-hop with Blacks and learned a few country songs from Whites.

I fell in love with jazz and lost myself to old rock and roll. I became a citizen of the world, and the world became my dance floor. But wait, there's more!

I ate food from every country as I traveled cross-country. I made new friends along every highway and along every byway. We lived the good life and became perplexed at the simultaneous beauty and ugliness of Life.

The Russians read us Tolstoy and danced the ballet while the modern leaders of Russia sought to bring about doomsday. The Persians read us Rumi and mystic stories of unity while the modern leaders of Iran spread strife in the Community. The Chinese people excelled at everything and earned first place while the modern leaders of China tried to steal first place.

And the Americans? Ah, the Americans. What can I say about that greatest of all Neighborhoods that made the world into one great Neighborhood?

The Americans clothed us in designer jeans and entertained us on big screens. They welcomed us openly with outstretched arms while our home countries expelled us and killed us with firearms.

The Americans showed us how to play together nicely and taught us the rules of Business concisely. They helped us trade in our Sectarianism and Fear for burgers and beer.

We experienced a Golden Age in the Community of Friendly Neighbors, until we didn't. The Americans soon forgot themselves and America descended into the Sectarianism and Fear from which it had once saved the world.

We scratched our heads in shock and bewilderment when the Americans began to bicker as everyone got sicker. They killed each other, one after another. They slurred and demurred, descending into the absurd. They retreated and cheated until all confidence was depleted. They passed the blame, spread the shame, and ruined their good name.

America split off into isolated Communities that labeled everyone else as "Outsiders." All of us Outsiders went back to our own neighborhoods and sang our songs and told our stories. Alone. Sometimes together. Not always with enough food and drink.

I took out my Explorer passport and decided to explore the neighborhoods in the Realm, hoping to find a Community where I would no longer be an Outsider. I wanted to feel welcome and at home, instead of unwelcome and alone.

I knocked on doors asking people if they would like to eat and drink with me. I thought maybe I could find a Community of fellow eaters and drinkers. So...

I knocked on a Vegan's door and invited him to a steakhouse. I couldn't understand why he shut the door to his house.

I served Neapolitan-style pizza to someone who was gluten-free. I couldn't understand why she rejected my meal even though it was free.

Then someone served me ice cream and I discovered the hard way that it makes me let off steam (not in a good way). So, I joined the Lactose-Free Community. But there's only so much time one can spend in that land of opportunity.

I needed to find a business community where I'd be looked at suitably and approvingly. And eat well without raising hell.

The next door I knocked on was answered by a man who looked friendly enough. I explained my situation and he invited me in. The house was filled with people who were eating and drinking well. I wanted to join them. The man served me a margarita. I noticed he had a bottle of whiskey on his shelf, so I asked him for a whiskey instead.

That must have offended him. He raised his eyebrows and glanced at the others in the house. They all turned their heads in unison toward me, looking at me angrily. They stared. I stared back. I gave in.

"Okay, fine! I'll take a margarita!"

"Too late. No margaritas for you."

"But why?"

"You don't deserve one. Margaritas are for Insiders. You're clearly an Outsider. You better get outta here quick, like, before we do something nasty."

Not wanting to antagonize the man and his angry mob any further, I got up and left the house. I went to the next house, confused as to why asking for whiskey would have elicited such an angry response. I wondered, *Is this stupid or am I crazy?* I couldn't understand how anything and everything caused so much offense to everyone in this Realm.

Word of my offenses must have spread throughout the Community because the people in the next house didn't even answer the door when I knocked. I continued knocking on doors unsuccessfully until I exhausted all the doors in the Community.

So I went to another Community. And then another. Everyone seemed to me as though they were angry, disgruntled, and offended. Nobody seemed interested in letting me in because I wasn't angry, disgruntled, and offended. Or so I thought at the time.

In one Community, they believed that women were men and men were women, and some people were neither men nor women. Then they wanted to talk about it nonstop publicly, privately, with kids and with adults. I said, "Fair enough. You can believe whatever you want to believe and talk about it publicly, privately, with kids and with adults. It's a free country. But can I believe whatever I want to believe? And if so, can I talk about it publicly, privately, with kids and with adults?"

They replied, "Absolutely not. We're the only ones who are allowed to believe what we want, and talk about what we want, publicly, privately, with kids and with adults." That didn't make any sense to me. I replied, "Why should one group of people have freedom of expression while other groups of people or belief systems get stifled? I think it's better to either stifle them all or liberate them all."

They canceled me.

I went to another Community where they believed that it's okay to stifle the voices of people who believe that women are men and men are women, and some people are neither men nor women. They said to me, "God created them male and female, so let no one change what God has made." I replied, "I think you're mixing up your Bible verses. From my understanding, God created people in his image, 'male and female, created he them.' To me, that reads as if God has masculine attributes and feminine attributes. He then bestowed all human beings with his attributes when he created them in his image. It's between God and the person he created whether their attributes are male or female. I think it's really none of your business or my business."

They canceled me.

I thought and thought about what to do next until I couldn't think anymore. I felt completely alone and entirely out of place.

It was as though I had somehow become an alien in my own country. Then I felt a light tap on my shoulder. I glanced back and was greeted by none other than The Chairman!

I asked what he was doing here, and he said that he was visiting some relatives. He then inquired about my Journey, and I told him many of the things that I had learned.

He asked me about my time in this Realm, and I told him I was having a tough time figuring out my place. It seemed as if I was destined to be an Outsider, but I couldn't accept that to be my fate. For the first time since my defeat in the Arena, I felt like a real loser.

I told him how I met various Communities and found them all to be very cliquish. They seemed to constantly talk about the things that made them different from me. They treated anyone who was different from them as Outsiders.

I didn't believe their differences were worth discussing, but they didn't want to discuss anything but their differences with me. I didn't want to label myself or separate myself from people who were different from me. I thought it strange that they did. I wondered why we couldn't all just eat and drink and sing and dance together, without labels. So they labeled me as an Outsider and treated me like a stranger.

I was apparently an Outsider because I didn't look like them, didn't talk like them, didn't walk like them, didn't drink like them, didn't believe like them, didn't *not* believe like them, didn't ask questions like them, or didn't *not* ask questions like them. Or because I didn't didn't didn't when I should've should've should've. Or because I did did did when I shouldn't shouldn't shouldn't.

Then I told The Chairman how I had come to really despise the Exhibitionists, and really anyone who was loud and obnoxious. The Exhibitionists remote-controlled their Communities from the Square of Modern Marketing. I was afraid I'd never be fully rid of them, in this or any other Realm.

I explained how I felt my position on just about anything was superior to other opinions voiced in this Realm. I told him how I couldn't deal with stupid people, and how I simply had no respect for people who voiced opinions on things about which they had no true knowledge.

I shared how I was thinking of requiring people to take an intelligence test in order to earn the privilege of interacting with me. I explained how I was proud of my Elitism and thought my Intellectual Superiority was worth admiration. Surely others would see it at some point in time, but I wasn't quite sure how to deal with them in the meantime. When I was nearly finished telling The Chairman about my experiences, he looked at me and asked, "Are you done yet?"

"Excuse me?"

"You sound like a lunatic."

"What do you mean?"

"You sound like a Stupid Arrogant Fool who's full of himself and can't wait to spend the rest of his life making love to himself."

I objected. He repeated his criticism of me. I objected again. He reminded me to pick my battles wisely. I glared at him, but he won the staring contest.

"Look," he said. "You're clearly frustrated. It seems like the people in this Realm have offended you, even though you're not willing to admit it. You seem angry, disgruntled, and offended, just like everyone else. If you don't like the Communities they've created here, why don't you just create your own?"

"My own Community?"

"Yes."

"How would that work?"

"Well, do you want other people to be a part of your Community, or would you rather live in your Community all by yourself?"

"Are you kidding?"

"No."

"Well, I suppose I want other people to be a part of my Community."

"Then you'll need to exchange your Intellectual Superiority for Intellectual Curiosity. You'll need to trade in your Arrogance for Reverence."

"Reverence?!"

"Yes. You need to respect your fellow human beings as much as you respect yourself. If you can't respect them, respect the God who created them. Do you believe in God? Or excuse me. Let me rephrase. Maybe you're too cool for school. Do you believe in The Great Spirit, The Universe, The Supreme Intelligence, The Force, The Goddess of Love, The Dude Who Created the Simulation, or whatever else people in your world call God these days?"

I looked at him blankly, slightly offended. Then I said, "Yes. I believe in God and I call him God."

At that, he reminded me of the words of Rumi, who said that the purpose of every trip is to meet the innermost presence of God as it lives in the people you encounter. The Chairman then shared how it was customary in Asia for businesspeople, and all people actually, to bow to one another out of respect for the Deity in the other person.

"Do you believe that God created all human beings, or just the ones who think like you?"

"Well, I believe that God created everyone."

"Right. You'd be Stupid to believe otherwise. Are you Stupid?"

"No."

"Good. Then stop acting Stupid. Just because someone doesn't think like you, that doesn't mean you have the right to feel as though you're better than them."

"But aren't I?"

The Chairman sighed and seemed to be getting annoyed with me. So I said, "Fine. You're right. I don't want to be Stupid or Arrogant. Any ideas on how I could improve?"

He looked at me skeptically and said there was someone whom he'd like for me to meet.

The Chairman introduced me to Empathy, who had apparently joined him on his visit to this Realm. She had dark skin, purple hair, and an infectious giggle that made even the most Stupid Arrogant Fools like me smile. Empathy encouraged me to be kind to everyone, even the Exhibitionists.

We bid The Chairman goodbye, and she led me to a neighborhood called the Community of Reformed Exhibitionists. There, Empathy explained to me the Story of the Exhibitionists: "Many are mentally ill," she informed me. "They refuse to get proper treatment. Many Exhibitionists have personality disorders that cause them to genuinely believe their own shit-filled Stories. Some are addicted to Attention, Jealousy, Drugs, and other mind-altering substances. Their relationships with those substances are, unfortunately, more important to them than their relationships with people."

Then she introduced me to Reformed Exhibitionists who had made the choice at some point in their Journey to Reform. They had discarded their masks, and I could see how they were actually beautiful human beings. Their ugliness and fakery had transformed into genuine beauty after they went through their

Reformation. Their features were distinctively attractive, their smiles were genuine, and their eyes were radiant. They smelled nice too.

Empathy then told me that I shouldn't insult Exhibitionists with angry words. Otherwise, I'd end up just like them. At the same time, however, I shouldn't allow them to bully me around. She warned, "They're like schoolyard bullies who'll keep pushing you around unless you find a way to stand up to them and minimize their Role in your life. Be Firm. Be Strategic. Use playful, challenging words, spoken truthfully.

"But always remember that bullies are people too. There's probably a reason why they became bullies in the first place. Be Reverent to the God who created them while limiting your exposure to them as much as you can. With a little luck, a very tiny percentage of them who are non-Fools may choose to Reform. But don't hold your breath!"

I nodded in agreement, although I still voiced my urge to trash-talk the Exhibitionists at every opportunity because I felt it "fair, fitting, and proper." She replied with a sigh and whispered softly, "Christ healed the blind and raised the dead, but the Fool he could not cure."

"Excuse me?"

"I quote those words whenever I find someone to be resistant to my lessons. They remind me that people will only allow me to accompany them on their Journey when the time is right for them. Perhaps the time isn't right for you. I'm really not sure if we're a good fit. Am I missing something?"

I could feel my face turning red. Empathy was using the same sales tactic on me that I had used on those mean little children who refused to allow me to accompany them earlier in my Journey. I decided to put aside my Arrogance and ask her nicely, very nicely, to reconsider.

"I'm sorry," I said. "I just have a real aversion to bullies because I've had some personal experience with them. I've seen first-hand the devastation they can cause with their disgusting lies and shit-filled Stories. I want to follow your lead. But honestly, it'll be a struggle for me as it relates to the Exhibitionists."

She looked at me compassionately, and tears welled up in her eyes. "My child," she said gently. "At some point, we'll need to talk about your personal experiences, and I'll introduce you to my sister. Her name is Forgiveness. But for now, I'll agree to work with you on one condition. Will you hold my hand and visit a few more neighborhoods with me?"

I agreed. Then Empathy took my hand, and together we knocked on doors that had previously been shut in my face. I learned that the guy who declined to serve me margaritas at his home did so because his little girl was killed in a drunk-driving accident by a man who drank whiskey.

The whiskey bottle was on his shelf as a reminder of that tragic incident. Anyone who asked for whiskey in his house was clearly an Outsider because they didn't know, or care to know, his family's story.

The margaritas he served at his home were hand-mixed with no alcohol and were simply a fancy name he gave to the limeade and lemonade he served his guests. It was an inside joke and one of the ways he coped with his family tragedy.

I apologized for my insensitivity and shed more than one tear as he shared photos of his beautiful little girl, who was robbed of Life at such an early age.

I observed Empathy as she knocked on door after door, listening to families tell their stories of violence, discrimination, bullying, and all sorts of human suffering. I was shocked at how similar the human grievances were, regardless of the Community.

I admired how gently she held their hands and how generously she gave them her shoulder to cry on. The tragedies visited upon many of my fellow humans, and the unrealistic expectations placed on them from childhood until now, were quite sad and oppressive, actually.

I began to realize how and why they became the way they did, and how and why they believed what they did. They were all Children of Life, yet they were somehow made to feel as though their Child of Life identity wasn't enough. They were always in search of new identities that felt more welcoming, as well as new Communities where they could feel at home.

So they created those Communities, and I was the Stupid Arrogant Fool who judged them. When we had finished hearing many of their stories, Empathy looked at me and signaled it was time to leave.

On our way to the next and final Community, she explained how everyone has a place in this Community of Friendly Neighbors and that "From the beginning of Time until now, people go where they feel most welcome. If people of a certain belief system or skin color or background feel welcome together, and unwelcome anywhere else, they'll stick together.

"If we are to have any hope of getting the Communities to interact productively with each other, or to dance with each other instead of shouting at each other, we need to listen to their concerns. We need to really hear what they're trying to say. Then we need to give up some of our own rigid, unrealistic expectations of them. Only then can we begin to heal the wounds that have been inflicted and create a thriving Community of Friendly Neighbors once again."

When she had finished her lessons, she asked me to share with her my Story. I struggled for words, and then I broke down in tears. I had not realized until now that that's what I was longing for all along. I simply wanted to be heard. To be accepted. To be loved. Just like all the others here in this Community of Friendly Neighbors. I said, "I really want to tell my Story and speak my Truth, but I'm afraid."

"What are you afraid of?"

"I'm afraid that people will bully me because I tend to think differently than they do. The atmosphere is so toxic and explosive right now that I simply don't want to get blown up if I speak up."

"Do you think you have something valuable to say? A Story that could benefit people?"

"Yes."

"Then isn't it true that you have a moral obligation to tell your Story?"

"How so?"

"Well, if someone could benefit from your Story, then you're deliberately not benefiting them if you hold back. What if your Story could make life better for just one person, and you fail to tell it because you're too afraid?"

I started to think about her question but then had to table my thoughts and our discussion for another time. We had arrived at our final destination, a Community that I had neglected to visit on my own.

Empathy led me to the Community of Family and Friends. I was greeted by home-cooked meals and fresh lemonade, like the kind my great-aunt used to make with a little orange blossom water mixed in. The tastes and aromas took me back to the lovely days and lovelier people who always made me feel at home. I ate and drank a lot, and my belly continued to grow.

I got reacquainted with many people in the Community of Family and Friends that I had lost touch with over the years. They seemed to have discovered on their Journeys many secrets of Life, which they generously shared with me.

One wise man extolled the virtues of "a crap and a nap" to keep Trouble from landing in my lap. I've heeded his advice on more than one occasion, especially on Sunday afternoons.

One wise woman advised me to "always remember there are people climbing beneath you and people climbing above you as you climb the Ladders of Life." If I remembered this truth, she advised, I could strive for excellence and also help those climbing after me at the same time.

She said this simple truth could help me to remain humble no matter how far I climb the Ladders of Life. That's because others can climb, have climbed, and will climb higher than me. In the cases where I need help climbing the Ladders, those who have already climbed above me can sometimes help me along. I've found her advice to be invaluable on many, many occasions.

I felt at home in this Community of Family and Friends and wondered whether it would be possible to create this feeling of home for others as they Journey through the Realms of Reality. I decided that nobody should be an Outsider, even if all they wanted to do was eat and drink, or sing and dance. I decided to create a Community for people who viewed themselves as StorySellers, regardless of any other labels they chose to wear or not wear.

Even StorySellers have to eat and drink. Why should we do it alone when we could do it together? We could be Intellectually Curious together and Reverent to the God who created our fellow human beings, all of whom are Children of Life. We could create an Oasis from the Exhibitionists and stand up to them with our playful, challenging words spoken truthfully. So that's what we did.

It came to pass that Empathy helped me to find and expand my Community of Friendly Neighbors. I embraced her, worked diligently with her, and followed her lead, leaving behind my Superiority Complex. I stopped looking at myself as an Outsider, and that's how I stopped being an Outsider. To be fair, I still struggle with the Exhibitionists, but that's another story for another time.

As for this story, at this time, it was time to share our lessons! I met up with a few of my fellow StorySellers, and we shared with each other what we had learned so far in our Journey.

One StorySeller had the distinction of always being the best-dressed person in the room, with her high-heeled boots, chic outfits, and citrus-colored shawls. Today she was wearing a sharp blue outfit with a bright orange shawl and matching orange boots. She flipped her hair back as she told us how she created long-term value for her business by focusing on what *won't* change in her Community. "The world is changing so fast," she said in her signature singsong voice. "But there is one thing that will never change—specifically, the humanity of each person in my Community. If I can find a way to connect with that humanity, I'll never be an Outsider." I found her insight to be extraordinarily valuable.

Another StorySeller had the distinction of being the most plainspoken, unassuming, down-to-earth multimillionaire you'd ever want to meet. He shared in his signature soft voice that everyone desires safety and acceptance. "We're all terrified of being Outsiders," he said. "You can build an incredible business by helping people in your Community feel safe and accepted when they work with you." I also found his insight to be invaluable.

All these things I learned in the Community of Friendly Neighbors, and more. Much, much more. But still, I felt something was lacking. I didn't want to spend the rest of my life here in this Community. I was getting anxious to continue on my Journey and see what more I could discover.

Up until now, I had raced my chariot in the Arena as a Warrior and explored the Blue Oceans of Life and Business as an Explorer. I made Magic with the Magicians and Ruled the Realm with the Rulers. I laughed with the Comedians and found my Community of Friendly Neighbors. But still, I hadn't found my Unique, Authentic Winning Story.

I wondered if I'd ever find it, or if I'd simply die trying. The trying part was okay, and I had certainly learned many lessons along the way. But I was not content. I wanted more. I needed more. So I decided to search for more.

I paid a visit to The Chairman in his Community. I asked him about the Great Contest in which he had promised to enroll me back when we were together in the Winner's Club. He replied that the Great Contest would be a completely new Journey for me. He reminded me that I must first complete this Journey through the Realms of Reality.

We shared more than a few stories, and he reminded me to always bring Empathy along whenever I journeyed through this Realm. He pointed out, "Empathy is more valuable than your Warrior glasses, your Explorer passport, your Magician hat, your Ruler Contract, and your Comedian platform combined."

We then bid each other farewell. I didn't realize it at the time, but that was the last time I'd see The Chairman on my Journey through the Realms of Reality.

And so it came to pass that I left the Community of Friendly Neighbors by making one last tragic mistake. I had taken my own Community for granted, not realizing that the people in it would not always be there.

Looking back at that moment, as I often have, I can't help but wonder whether I spent my time in the Community of Friendly Neighbors as wisely as I should have. I vowed to do better. I vowed to enjoy each moment with my Community and to treasure the people in my Community before it's too late. That's a vow that I still strive to honor to this day.

As for the next phase in my Journey, I was destined to visit the Studio of Artists. Little did I know that I'd become an Artist of sorts, or the crazy kind of Art that I would create. I had no clue that Artistry was in my blood or that I'd actually enjoy the process of creating it.

As for the people I'd meet, well, that's another story, and it's time I told it.

CHAPTER 8

The Studio of Artists

THE MISSION:

Chisel away with us at the Imperfect until it becomes Magnificent...or fade away in our Prison of Insignificance.

THE SIGN AT THE ENTRANCE OF THE ARTIST'S STUDIO READ:

You are the Artists, the Mirrors through which we see ourselves.

May the reflections in your Mirrors show us the best version of ourselves.

You are the Creators, the ones who Create the Future.

May the Future you Create be filled with joy and laughter.

You are the Builders, the ones who reach towering heights.

Help us build each other up as we live out our days and nights.

You are the Composers, the Writers of our Destiny.

May you always be free to do your work successfully.

You are the Virtuosos and Valued Experts at your Craft.

May your value multiply as you advance in every Craft.

You are the Respected Maestros and Masters of the Universe.

May the Universe be generous to you and always fill your purse.

You are the Artists, the Mirrors through which we see ourselves.

May the reflections in your Mirrors be the best version of ourselves.

Let me back up a little. Just when I thought my belly couldn't get any bigger, I was introduced to the most magnificent spread of Italian food I had ever seen. Pasta and antipasto served with Barbaresco and Barolo wine. Followed by Tuscan bread dipped in olive oil and Neapolitan-style pizza served with even more wine. Followed by a delicious spread of meats and cheeses, topped off by cannoli and limoncello for dessert. But wait, there's more!

I forgot to mention that prior to being served all this delicious Italian food, I had shared a magnificent Lebanese breakfast in the Community of Friendly Neighbors with The Chairman. Our breakfast included such mouthwatering delicacies as salted tomatoes, man'oushi (flatbread topped with za'atar spice), and knafeh b'jibneh (pastry filled with molten cheese and topped with orange blossom syrup).

As we bid each other farewell in the Community, The Chairman suggested I visit a friend of his in the next Realm over, who went by the simple name of The Artist. The Artist, he warned me, may seem distracted because she was always in the midst of an all-consuming project.

My mission, he reminded me from our time together in Orientation, would be to chisel away with her at the Imperfect until it becomes Magnificent. Otherwise, he cautioned, The Artist and her friends may throw me into their Prison of Insignificance, where I would very likely never escape.

He suggested I take a bottle of wine and a bouquet of flowers to present as a gift to The Artist. But not just any wine or any flowers. The Artist only drank fine wine, preferably Italian. She also appreciated when people showed attention to detail in the type of flowers they selected. The Chairman suggested purple roses, as they would indicate a proper sense of fascination with and adoration for The Artist and her magnificent creations.

I followed his advice, armed myself with fine wine and purple roses, and visited the Realm of Artists. Apparently, the Artists in this Realm lived in the basements of what seemed to be large Palaces. There was one Artist allowed in each basement. I knocked on the door of the Palace where The Artist who knew The Chairman lived.

She didn't answer the door at first, so I followed up with several more knocks, evenly spaced. I didn't want her to think I was haphazard in my knocking. I also wanted to prove to myself that there was a scientific method to knocking on doors and following up. They say that follow-up is more art than science, but I wanted to inject some science into my art to see what happened.

Soon enough—though I'm not sure whether it was due to the art or science of my evenly spaced knocks—The Artist answered her door. She was a tall, gorgeous blond, and her body was perfectly formed. She was definitely more art than science. I was absolutely stunned by her exquisite beauty. She wore hardly any clothes, which made me blush.

She accepted my gifts and invited me in. I didn't know whether to run away or accept her invitation. "I won't bite, darling," she said in a dreamy voice. "Besides, my husband has cooked up a storm, and I'm famished. Please come in, and share a bite with us."

I cautiously entered the Palace, admiring every inch of her as I inched my way in. She led me through the spacious kitchen, where the most delicious aromas tantalized my senses. Even so, the aromas weren't enough to distract all my senses from being completely focused on her.

I followed The Artist through the Palace and onto the terrace, where the abundant spread of food I mentioned earlier was being served. There were several guests seated at a long table, all of them wearing very little clothing.

The Artist introduced me to her husband, who was equally as chiseled and beautiful as she was. He wasn't wearing a shirt, and he invited me to take off my shirt and join the other guests at the table. I objected due to the size of my belly. "I'm a little out of shape," I said. "I don't think you really want to see me with no shirt." He replied that the human body is magnificent regard-less of its shape.

I didn't know whether to laugh out loud at his ridiculous attempt at humor or whether he was actually serious. I kept my shirt on. After the magnificent meal, during which I got more than my fill of pasta and wine, The Artist, her husband, and their guests invited me to join them in their Basement Studio.

The Artist was apparently unlike any of the other Artists in the Realm. The Rulers of the Realm had given her the freedom to do things her way. She was what they called a Master Artist.

One of the things she chose to do differently from others in the Realm was to work with other Artists as a team instead of working alone. Apparently, the guests I had become acquainted with during the magnificent meal were members of her team.

As we reached the Basement Studio, I saw the aforementioned sign at the entrance. Then I saw a large sculpture in the middle of the Studio that appeared to be half-finished. The sculpture was part natural stone and part blown glass. To me, it evoked both strength and fragility. Natural beauty with the stamp of human genius. The Artist called her sculpture *Modern Society as It Could Be*. She had somehow, here in her basement, managed to capture the essence of humanity in one magnificent piece of art.

Modern Society as It Could Be was colorful and radiant, reflecting the rays of the sun as they seeped through the window. It was as if I was looking through an incandescent prism, through which I could see myself and all of humanity. The answers to many of life's most perplexing questions seemed to bounce around the room, illuminated by the brilliance of the sculpture.

The Artist explained that she and her team had been working on this sculpture for many years. She said, "In three days' time, this sculpture, which is currently Imperfect, will be made Magnificent." Then she invited me to join them in chiseling away at the Imperfect. So I did. Sort of.

I found a chisel and began to chip away with the other Artists. I yearned to put my stamp on this magnificent piece of art. I wanted to contribute my part. No, I needed to contribute. I simply followed my intuition, even as the Voice had instructed me to do long ago when it first sent me on this Journey. Somehow, the chiseling came naturally to me. I only needed to believe in myself, pick up the chisel, and get to work. I felt no fear in that moment, only intense focus. The world and all my cares melted away as I lost myself to my work.

However, I found that my clothes were getting quite dirty with the dust created from chiseling away at the sculpture. A few tiny shards of glass apparently broke off as well, unbeknownst to me. Every time I dusted off my clothes, the dust and tiny shards of glass would fly into the faces of the other Artists, distracting them from their work. They would look at me with a sense of frustration. Then they'd look at each other and shrug.

After a few hours of chiseling away at the Imperfect, my shirt had become soaked with sweat, causing the dust to attach itself to me, along with the tiny shards of glass. They were caked on me so thick that large pieces would fly off and strike my fellow artists in the face whenever I made a large or sudden movement.

This, of course, caused even more frustration, more shrugs, and more dirty looks. Just as the Artists were ready to explode in their anger toward me, two large unhappy fellows entered the room. The first went by the name of Mediocrity, and the second by the name of Perfectionism. They began to distract the Artists with nonsense and verbal abuse.

But I'm getting ahead of myself. Let's go back and talk about my shirt. At this point, as I mentioned, my shirt had been soaked with sweat and caked with dust and tiny shards of glass. The Artist came up to me and said I must strip down if I am to continue working with her and her team in the Studio.

I objected, stating that in my experience and in my world, such an ultimatum would be considered sexual harassment. Upon my saying so, she erupted in laughter so loud that the vibrations caused the light fixtures in the room to start shaking. The other Artists joined in, and before long the entire room had exploded in laughter at the apparent Fool before them.

After the laughing died down, The Artist looked at me and said, quite seriously, "Nobody wants to have sex with you. Calm down, lover boy. We're focused on work here. If you wanna play around, you're welcome to do so, just not in my Studio. The reason we have very little clothing on is out of respect for ourselves and each other. The clothes in this Studio are like outer coverings that do nothing but gather dust and distract us from doing our work. The only way we can turn the Imperfect into the Magnificent is to be our truest authentic selves. No artificial coverings if they can be avoided. This means we have to be vulnerable and not worry about covering up our 'large bellies,' as you would call them."

I replied defensively, "Well, that's easy for you to say, given the impeccable state of your body, but my body isn't perfect like yours. I need lots of clothes to cover up my imperfections."

She answered, "Lover boy, your artificial coverings are preventing you from doing your work. Either strip down to your truest self or get the hell out of my Studio."

"That's harsh."

"That's Reality."

"Fine."

"Fine?"

"Yes, fine. I'll show you my belly."

And with that, I took off my shirt, puffed out my chest, and let my gigantic belly hang out. I picked up my chisel and got back to work, making a mental note to get myself into shape. I thought to myself, *If I truly must show my belly and be my truest self, why not become my best self and downsize my belly? It seems like the decent thing to do out of respect for myself and my fellow Artists. After all, nobody wants to look at a huge belly when so many other viable options are readily available.*

So, now that we've settled that, let's stop talking about my shirt and my belly. Instead, let's talk about Mediocrity and Perfectionism. After making his grand entrance, Mediocrity approached us. He smelled like a distillery and had pieces of food stuck in his scraggly beard. The guy looked absolutely gross. I wondered when he last took a shower. He looked us up and down and then said, "Stop working. There's no need to continue. Everything is fine just as it is. I'm fine. You're fine. We're all fine. Let's go drink some fine wine!"

The Artists seemed annoyed at Mediocrity, and they shot him dirty looks. Some of them even put up their hands and tried to cover their faces so as not to see his ugliness. He was quite repulsive. I joined in their annoyance and also gave him a dirty look, though I soon found myself gawking at his hideous appearance.

Clearly, Mediocrity didn't understand what we were doing. He was trying to distract us with tales of leisure, reminding us that abundant food and drink were just upstairs. We resisted. He persisted.

Somehow, we managed to blow him off and continue working. Perfectionism lurked in the background, and I had no idea what he was planning. Perfectionism was quite the opposite of Mediocrity. He was clean-shaven and smelled like designer cologne. He wore a custom-fitted blue suit, probably Italian, and a crisp white shirt with diamond cuff links. He looked dashing in his colorful silk tie with a matching handkerchief tucked in his suit pocket. Not a hair on his head was out of place. He looked down at us and scrunched his nose as if we smelled terrible, which we probably did due to our sweatiness.

We worked all day and half the night until our hands became bloodied and our bodies dripped with sweat. The dust from our work had packed into large brown piles on the floor as it mixed with our sweat and mingled with our blood.

As we were nearing the point of exhaustion, The Artist approached us and suggested we call it a day. At that point, Perfectionism began to harass us and slur our progress. "You'll never finish," he chided. "You simply don't have what it takes. Your work sucks." The Artist looked at him and stared him down. He backed off. I remembered what Empathy had told me about bullies and how the best approach is to simply stand up to them.

The Artist was clearly well acquainted with that lesson, and she applied Empathy's lessons to herself and her team. I was glad to be under her protection. Or so I thought. Little did I know that my temporary presence in this Realm would soon take on a more permanent nature, and that The Artist would not be so protective the next time Perfectionism harassed me.

After that first day of hard work, we cleaned the Studio, took showers, and quickly fell asleep on the floor of the adjacent basement bedrooms. When we awoke the next day, we found that someone had defaced our sculpture and toppled it over. The pieces of our work were shattered all over the floor of the Studio, and there was no way of repairing the damage. It was devastating. We were all in shock.

We had no idea how this had happened, or why. Neither did we know who did it. We were all apparently in such a deep sleep that not a single one of us had seen the intruder or heard the mayhem that occurred in the middle of the night.

The Artist, who I thought would be fuming with anger, was rather stoic about the incident. She said that true Artists find their joy in the work itself, not in the results of the work. She quoted from the scriptures of various religions and said something about dedicating our work to God and not being attached to the results.

From the Holy Bible, she quoted:

> The Lord gives and the Lord takes away. Blessed be the name of the Lord... And whatsoever you do, do it with your whole heart, as to the Lord, and not unto men.

From the Bhagavad Gita, she quoted:

> You have the right to work, but never to the fruit of work. You should never engage in action for the sake of reward... [T]hose who are motivated only by desire for the fruits of action are miserable, for they are constantly anxious about the results of what they do.

From the Dhammapada, she quoted:

> Do not give your attention to what others do or fail to do; give it to what you do or fail to do... When you attain victory over yourself, not even the gods can turn it into defeat.

Paraphrasing the words of Buddha, she told us:

> Suffering happens when we cling to something we want. But life always changes, and we often don't get what we want. Therefore, in order to stop suffering, we must simply let go. We must stop clinging to unfulfilled desires and expectations. Instead, focus on thinking well, speaking well, and acting well...now in this moment.

Then she told us a story from a novel called *The Fountainhead*. The book was written many years ago by the American thinker and atheist Ayn Rand. Her main character, Howard Roark, created magnificent architecture and didn't care in the least bit about the results of his work. That's because he did his work, not for his clients, not for fame or fortune, not to serve God, but for the simple reason that he enjoyed it. He was doing what he was born to do in the way he was born to do it.

After quoting these scriptures and telling us these stories, she encouraged us to pick up our chisels and get back to work, not for the sake of reward, but for the Meaning and Joy we'd find in the work itself.

I hardly understood the meaning of all her quotes and stories. In fact, I seemed to be angrier than her at the injustice of the situation. I remarked that it certainly didn't seem fair, especially given the fact that she had spent years of her life on this project. She would now be required to start again from scratch. She replied that an Artist creates Art for the same reason that a bird flies. It simply cannot be helped, regardless of the results of the endeavor.

Again, I hardly understood her meaning, and I mentioned that it seemed time for me to go. I thanked her for her hospitality and got up to leave. She seemed very puzzled and said, "Not so fast, darling. You came into this Realm voluntarily, but you cannot leave without creating something Magnificent. Otherwise, you'll spend the rest of your days in the Prison of Insignificance."

"Excuse me?" I replied.

"Didn't The Chairman tell you about the Rules of this Realm?" she answered.

I stuttered back, "Well, um, yeah...yes, he did. He said I would need to chisel away at the Imperfect until it becomes Magnificent. Otherwise, you may throw me into your Prison of Insignificance, where I would very likely never escape."

"And?"

"Well, I did help out. I worked all day and half the night yesterday."

"And?"

"And what?"

"Did you make the Imperfect Magnificent?"

"Uh, no."

"Well?"

"Well, what?"

"You haven't paid your dues yet."

"I don't understand."

"I'm sure you do."

"I'm sure I don't."

"Look, darling. You can't come into this Realm and leave projects undone. It's simply not allowed. Follow me."

She took my hand and led me out of the basement, out of the Palace, and into the street. We walked down the road toward a gigantic building surrounded by barbed wire. "This is the

Prison of Insignificance," she informed me. "Option 1, complete your mission and chisel away at the Imperfect until it becomes Magnificent. Option 2, spend the rest of your life in this Prison of Insignificance. Are we clear now?"

I looked at her, slightly confused, and said, "But I'm not an Artist."

She replied, "Everyone is an Artist. Most escape their calling and end up in this Prison. The smart ones, the brave ones, do their work and create their Art. Are you smart and brave or stupid and cowardly?"

"Well, I think I'm smart, and I try to be brave."

"Then don't be stupid and don't be cowardly. Pick up your chisel and get to work."

"Where?"

"Look around you, darling. What do you see?"

I looked around. Aside from the enormous Prison, this Realm was filled with Palaces. Each Palace had its own Basement Studio. There were signs at the Palace entrances with the names of their Studios. I began reading off to The Artist some of the names that I saw: "The Studio of Music, The Studio of Computer Programming, The Studio of Sales, The Studio of Operations, The Studio of Leadership..."

The Artist interrupted me and said, "Very good, darling. I'm glad to see you know how to read. Now pick your Studio and get to work."

I wasn't too happy with her tone, but she certainly seemed to know what she was doing. So I asked her, "Can I go back with you to your Studio?"

"No," she quickly replied.

"Why not?" I asked.

"You're not ready," she answered.

"When will I be ready?"

"When you stop talking about your belly. It's not enough to simply show your belly and act like an authentic Artist. You must master the Art of your profession with the skill and discipline of a true Artist. You must do your work—minute after minute, hour after hour, day after day—without complaining. You must do this until the days become months, and the months turn into years, and the years turn into decades of creating your Art. You must master your profession to be a Master Artist. I'm not just any Artist, you know, and neither are the people who work with me. We are Master Artists. If you want to join us in our Studio and live in our Palace, then you must become a Master Artist as well."

I replied, "Fair enough. I'm in. I can do this."

She said, "Good. I know you can do this. Otherwise, The Chairman wouldn't have sent you to me. I told him I was looking for Artists who could become Masters. He only sends me the ones he believes in, and apparently, he believes in you."

Then she turned and walked away. Back to her Studio. Back to her Palace. I wandered the streets for a bit and picked the Studio that I felt would be most suitable given the skills that I had acquired so far on my Journey. There, I began to chisel away at the Imperfect until it became Magnificent.

I was continually harassed by Mediocrity and Perfectionism like all the other Artists in the Realm. However, I remembered Empathy and applied her lessons to myself, the same way that The Artist had applied Empathy's lessons to herself and her team.

Many lessons I learned in the Studio of Artists, until one day the Imperfect stone sculpture I had been working on for so long became, to me, Magnificent. That's because I was working on a sculpture that told a story, the story of one particular chapter of my life. The story was chiseled in stone because it had already taken place. Nothing I could say or do would change that.

I realized the sculpture was finished when I ran my hands across it and felt the contrast of its sharp edges and smooth surfaces. The sharp edges represented the rough experiences of that chapter in my life while the smooth surfaces represented how everything seemed to turn out just fine in the end.

I instinctively knew the Imperfect had become Magnificent when I ran my hands across the sculpture and realized that nothing more could be added or taken away from that chapter of my life. It had enough sharp edges and smooth surfaces to fill an entire chapter. It was time for me to move on.

Meaning and Joy visited me that day, and we danced our celebratory dance around the finished sculpture. I turned on my music once again, the very same music that some would find boring and eclectic. But I wasn't dancing for them around their sculpture. I was dancing for me around my sculpture.

Of course, Perfectionism didn't understand, not in the least bit. He had no appreciation for true art or beauty. He harassed me at every moment as my work neared its conclusion. "The goal of art," I told him, "is delight, not perfection." But his limitations could not grasp how the Imperfect can simply *be* Magnificent.

So I instructed him further. "Art becomes Magnificent when it serves its purpose. When it delights. When it simultaneously reflects the image of its creator and the image of the one for whom it is created. The two images become as one, dancing in delight for their own pleasure. Dancing in the light of the Imperfect as it transforms itself into the Magnificent."

His reply was simply, "You're weird. That's weird. All you Artists are weird. I don't understand your poetry. So I prefer to make a mockery. Of you, and everything you do. You'll never be good enough, though you think you're hot stuff. I'm gonna harass you and your entire crew. Until the sun stops shining bright or you stop creating delight."

I answered simply, "You're weird. That's weird. And I'm gonna go now."

So I did. I rejected Perfectionism and presented my work to the rest of the Artists in the Realm. Some cheered. Some jeered. Some thought my work was weird. But that's okay. I didn't do my work for them. I did it for me. I began to understand what

The Artist told me about dedicating my work to God and not being attached to the results.

I decided to visit The Artist in her Studio before I exited the Realm. She was as beautiful as ever and welcomed me with open arms. This time, I hugged her, unashamedly, and it wasn't a sexual thing. Her husband served us another incredible Italian meal. This time, I was more disciplined as I worked my way through it.

The other Artists and I exchanged stories of how we rejected Mediocrity and Perfectionism, and how we put those bullies in their place. I felt as though I somehow belonged here, in this Realm of Artists, but I also knew that I must continue on my Journey.

I shared with the Artists some of the lessons I had learned in their Realm. Lessons about doing the work, being a professional, and finding fulfillment in the act of creating.

The Artist took my hand and led me to the edge of the terrace. She pointed up at the sun, which was starting to set. Then she said, "The Genius of Humankind is like a sun that casts shadows as it rises and sets. Some people live in the shadow of their own Genius, running away from it at every opportunity. Those are the ones who end up in the Prison of Insignificance.

"The ones who don't run away from their Genius are true Artists like you and me. We do our work in the light of the Genius who created us. We take pleasure in our work and dedicate it to our God, in whichever form we worship him. Which type of Genius are you? The kind who lives in the shadows or the kind who lives in the light?"

I replied that I strive to live in the light. "Very good," she said. "You're now ready to continue your Journey and visit the Academy of Scholars. It's right up that mountain." She pointed to the mountain range in the distance and said that all Artists must, at some point in their Journey, make their pilgrimage to the Academy.

"As you ascend that mountain," she warned, "the air will become more difficult to breathe, and you may feel yourself to be inadequately prepared. Those feelings are normal. No one is ever ready to climb the mountain, but all must do so in due time."

I was grateful for her warning and toasted her and her team with one final glass of wine before I left. I only wish now that someone had given me an instruction manual for what happened next.

CHAPTER 9

The Academy of Scholars

THE MISSION:

Help us find the Truth...or remain lost and forgotten on the never-ending Road to Nowhere.

I FOUND MYSELF AT THE FOOT OF THE MOUNTAIN OF SCHOLARS greeted by a sign that read:

> May all seekers of Knowledge make haste to climb this Mountain.
>
> At its peak you'll find our Academy and its life-giving Fountain.
>
> The Knowledge you'll drink from our Fountain will refresh you in many ways.
>
> It will nourish and sustain you through the hardest of your days.
>
> You'll discover ancient Truths that have modern applications.
>
> These Truths may shake your old beliefs to their foundations.
>
> Keep an open mind and stay ever-curious.
>
> Don't be shy to explore the mysterious.
>
> Try not to overanalyze when you meet Useless Data.
>
> Try not to be deceived by One-Sided Stories and Dogma.
>
> You'll meet these hideous creatures in the form of a nasty Shape-Shifter.
>
> He'll try to trap you on the Road to Nowhere, with a sigh and with a whisper.

Take heed not to get duped by that liar, and stay ever-watchful.

Remain inquisitive, ask many questions, and don't be bashful.

Search diligently for the Truth, and soon enough you'll find it.

The Truth will always appear to you when you are ready to mind it.

As I began my ascent up the Mountain of Scholars, toward their Academy, I did feel overwhelmed and inadequate, as The Artist had forewarned me. The higher I climbed, the more apprehensive I felt. I wondered whether I'd even gain admittance into the Academy or whether the Scholars would turn me away. When I finally made it to the peak of the Mountain, the Academy of Scholars appeared before me like a Light on a Hill. Except it wasn't a hill. It was a mountain. Many mountains.

The Academy was expansive. It spanned across several mountain ranges, connected by Bridges of Learning. Instead of being just one Academy, the Academy was more like a federation of many Academies. The main campus, however, was located here on this mountaintop. I was awestruck.

I felt myself being pulled toward the Academy, as if it were a magnet and I was being magnetized. It was unlike any feeling I had experienced on my Journey so far. As I made my way toward the entrance, I noticed a massive Gate.

The Gate resembled the first Gate that I walked through when I first entered into the Realms of Reality. It was tall, as if reaching up to heaven, yet narrow and crooked as if reaching down to hell. It was wrapped with thorns and roses all around. Again, I felt as though this Gate was custom-designed to simultaneously entice and repel people like me.

As I walked through the Gate, into the Academy, I was careful not to cut my hand on the thorns, but I couldn't help doing so. Regardless, I allowed the fragrance of the beautiful roses to dazzle my senses. A feeling of nostalgia washed over me.

What greeted me on the other side of the Gate was a quiet green square with a large fountain in its center. It felt as though I was coming home, yet I had no recollection of this place. The square was filled with flowers and hedges arranged neatly in order. It very much resembled an English garden.

I walked toward the fountain in the middle of the square and was mesmerized by its swirling waters, which spoke to me in their swishing voice. "Jump in," the waters beckoned to me. "Splash around and drink to your heart's delight!"

So I did! I jumped into the Fountain and splashed around like a little child. I giggled with delight and began drinking the water of the Fountain, which refreshed me after my long trek up the mountain. The more I drank, the more I wanted to drink. Just as I was about to take another huge gulp, I heard someone calling my name. I looked back and saw a man standing on the edge of the Fountain, trying to get my attention.

He looked like a professor type. He wore thick glasses and had gray hair and a long beard. He carried a book and wore a long black robe that covered his clothing. He smelled nice too. I could tell that he was wearing my favorite cologne.

"Welcome!" he said in a deep baritone voice. "We've been waiting for you."

"You have?"

"Yes. The Chairman told us you'd be paying us a visit, and I'm glad you finally made it."

"You know The Chairman?"

"Yes, of course. He singled you out, you know. Not everyone catches his attention. But for some reason, he knew you'd make it here. He told us to take real good care of you once you arrive. I see that you've splashed around here in the Fountain of Knowledge already."

I grinned, sheepishly.

"Come on, there'll be plenty of time for that later. You'll need to dry off and get dressed. There are some people I'd like for you to meet."

He then pointed to a building across the green square that was labeled Scholar Orientation. He instructed me to go to the front desk, where I'd be handed a key to my room. He told me a fresh set of clothes would be waiting for me on the bed. And a Scholar's Robe, which I should wear to cover my nakedness and acknowledge I have much to learn. He told me to wear it and then meet him back here in the English gardens after I freshened up.

I followed his instructions, and before long I found myself back in the gardens feeling ready to take on the world again. Or at the very least, I felt ready to explore the Academy.

The man who first greeted me extended his hand and said, "Now, for a proper introduction. You can call me The Professor. I will be your guide in this Academy." I nodded in agreement, and we went off on a tour. The Professor introduced me to all sorts of interesting people.

I met Philosophers who were wiser than Solomon because they either had no woman or had somehow managed to find a way to keep one woman happy. I marveled at their wisdom (and still do to this day).

I met Priests and Priestesses who wore red robes and adorned themselves with all manner of jewels. They dazzled me with their spiritual stories of love and unity. "Take pleasure in meaningful work," they instructed me, "even as God took pleasure in his meaningful work of creating you."

I met Prophets and Poets who wore pure white linen and found hidden meanings in everything. They told me, "When you discover Truth in one domain of Life, do not hesitate to apply it in another domain. In this manner, you can find Truth everywhere."

I met Academics and Practitioners who wore plain clothes and blue collars. They were all experts at their chosen professions. They advised, "The most basic duty of any Scholar is to figure out how to apply Truth practically, pragmatically, and punctually. Otherwise, all your searching and all your finding will have been done in vain."

Then I met a Teacher who had spent his entire life and career teaching just one student. That student grew up to teach the world. "Never begrudge your work or think it to be insignificant," the Teacher instructed me. "For you'll never know the long-term impact of your kindness or unkindness as the case may be."

I met Warriors and Explorers, Magicians and Rulers, Comedians and Artists. They had all made the pilgrimage, like me, to the Academy of Scholars.

They wanted to learn and become experts at their craft, so they enrolled in the Academy as Lifelong Students. I asked one of the Students what it took to become a Scholar. She replied that true Scholars don't see themselves as Scholars. They simply see themselves as Lifelong Students.

They generously share their findings with others. That's why others call them Scholars. But to themselves and to each other, they are simply Lifelong Students. They learn what they can, from whomever they can. They do this whenever they can. "But there will come a day," she said, "when you will graduate. In the meantime, let's get a bite to eat!"

Then she invited me to join her and her friends to share a meal with them. So I did. Then we started telling jokes. Lots of jokes.

One joke that I didn't find very funny was when I was asked to mediate a truce between two extremely argumentative factions within the Academy. They were called the Optimists and the Pessimists. Their argument centered around the very nature of humanity and the origin of our species.

The Pessimists believed that people were born in darkness, in the City of Dreams. When people's Dreams shatter and die, they become enlightened enough to enter into the Realms of Reality.

The key to Life, according to the Pessimists, is to not have Dreams in the first place. This way you'll never be disappointed when your Dreams shatter and die, as all Dreams invariably do.

The Optimists, on the other hand, believed that people were born enlightened in the Realms of Reality. They experience tragedies and hardships that cause them to retreat into the City of Dreams.

The key to Life, according to the Optimists, is for people to leave their City of Dreams and go back into the Realms of Reality in which they were born. There, they'll become the enlightened Children they once were.

Both viewpoints seemed to have valid arguments, but the Optimist viewpoint seemed to me the more valid of the two. So I sided with the Optimists. I apparently made a good choice—the Optimists rewarded me with an incredible meal that consisted of Asian food, sushi, and sake. Lots of sake.

On another occasion, as a sort of cruel hazing ritual, I was asked to define for the Scholars the meaning of Truth. I replied that Truth is whatever allows you to become the best version of yourself and create the most value for others, without lying to yourself or others.

That was apparently the correct answer. Until it wasn't. Many of the Scholars jeered at my answer and threw the Book at me. Which Book? All of them. They seemed to find conflicting Truth in all the Books of the Realm. The mixed messages in all their Books were so confusing that many Scholars literally went crazy. They developed extreme viewpoints and Superiority Complexes.

They banned Empathy from their midst, and she became persona non grata in the Academy. The Extremists truly believed themselves to be better than everyone who didn't share their extremist viewpoints.

The Extreme Right Wingers said, "Truth is whatever we say it is because we know God and he speaks to us. Thus says the Lord, do things our way because it's the only way!"

Then the Extreme Left Wingers replied, "Truth is whatever we say it is because we know God and he speaks to us. Thus says the Lord, do things our way because it's the only way!"

The two sides couldn't agree on the meaning of Truth! Both invoked the name of God, calling him different names and creating him in their own image. They built a Dark Temple to their God and burned Dark Incense in their Temple. They tried to envelop the Realm in the Darkness emanating from their Dark Temple.

Then they invited the Shape-Shifter to join them as a guest speaker in their Temple. The Shape-Shifter was a nasty fellow, and he reeked with smoke and shit. Cigarette smoke, that is. I'm not exactly sure what flavor of shit.

I could smell the foul odor of the Shape-Shifter as he approached. It made his movements quite predictable, actually. His mission in life, apparently, was to blow smoke up people's asses, distracting them from the pursuit of Truth. That's why he smelled so nasty.

The Shape-Shifter took many forms and disguises. That's why, unsurprisingly, his name became the Shape-Shifter. Prior to the Modern Age, he was known by other names. The ancient Africans called him Shetani, and he was known in Western cultures as simply Satan or the Devil.

His home was located down the road from the Academy and had the confusing name of Nowhere. Many Scholars who get frustrated or confused in the Academy find themselves walking down the Road to Nowhere, with no recollection of how they got there.

After the Extremists invited the Shape-Shifter into their Dark Temple, they asked him for validation and help in spreading their Darkness. "Tell us the story we want to hear," they implored. "Create Dark Stories of Lies that we can spread across the Realm."

The Shape-Shifter gladly obliged and did what he does best. He used Distorted Religion, One-Sided Stories, and lots of Useless Data to blow smoke up everyone's asses. This further solidified their positions, fueled their flames, and created even more Darkness in the Realm.

When he took the disguise of Distorted Religion, he put on red priestly robes and told stories called Dogma. His Stories of Dogma told Scholars that their belief system was the only Truth. It discouraged the exploration of other viewpoints. When he had converted many with his Stories of Dogma, he changed shapes again.

He transformed himself into a cable news anchor and became One-Sided Story. He spliced together various sound bites, video footage, and half-quotes, taking them all out of context to weave sinister One-Sided Stories. These One-Sided Stories deceived the Scholars in many ways that were destructive to themselves and the Realm.

Then he changed shapes again into a handheld tablet and took on the form of Useless Data. He threw at the Scholars many different Stories: Too Much Information, Too Little Information, Fake News, Real News, Data with No Context, and Context with No Data. He dared the Scholars to decipher the meaning of all these Stories and find meaning in them, which many tried to do in vain.

Many Scholars became confused and frustrated by all the Darkness being manufactured by the Shape-Shifter and his Extremists. They left the Academy in droves and ended up lost and forgotten on the never-ending Road to Nowhere, which I'm sure was the Shape-Shifter's intention all along.

As for me, I tried my best to stay out of the conflict and avoid the Darkness altogether. In fact, I did for a while. Until I didn't. When the Darkness became too much, I decided to speak up for the Moderates. The quiet ones like me, whose voices were being drowned by all the Darkness being manufactured by the Extremists and the Shape-Shifter.

We believed the Extremists were completely out of touch with Reality. So we embraced our own Reality. We created Stories of Truth to combat the Dark Stories of Lies that they were spreading. We told our Stories to the Shape-Shifter directly, refuting his lies point by point. We then told our Stories to our fellow Scholars, and really anyone who would listen.

"The mission of a Scholar," we advocated, "is to search for the Truth. To find the Truth. To teach the Truth. How can you search for something when you think you've already found it? How can you find something if you stop searching? How can you teach something without understanding the perspective of the one whom you are trying to teach?

"The true calling of the Scholar, therefore, is to be Moderate. To resist the urge of extreme viewpoints that are exclusive of the Reality of others. To never stop searching for new ideas. To be open to new perspectives. To continuously find and teach new and higher Truths."

The Extremists and the Shape-Shifter gnashed their teeth and jeered at us, but we were undeterred. In fact, by speaking *our* Truth, we realized that the vast majority of Scholars in the Realm agreed with us. You see, our Truth included practical lessons from all the world's religions, minus the Dogma. It included multidimensional stories that acknowledge the complexity of the human experience and the inherent diversity in all our viewpoints. Instead of sound bites taken out of context and mounds of Useless Data, we produced thoughtful step-by-step guides, entertaining stories, and rhymes—lots and lots of rhymes to help our fellow Scholars find their Truth and live it.

We became known as the Silent Majority, and then as simply the Majority. We gave a voice to those who felt they were voiceless as we advocated for Moderation and Reason. We found strength we didn't know we had, and we took back control of *our* Realm from the Right-Wing and Left-Wing Extremists who were destroying it with their nonsense.

The Darkness fled from us as quickly as we chased it away. We liberated ourselves from the influences of the Dark Temple and became Free Thinkers. Then we learned whatever we could, from whomever we could, whenever we could.

The Genius of God and the humans he created shone brightly in the Academy once again. It illuminated many Truths. Practical Truths helped us become the best versions of ourselves and create value for others. Spiritual Truths inspired us and gave meaning to our human lives. Political Truths showed us how to safeguard our own Freedom by ensuring that Freedom applies equally to everyone.

And so it came to pass that I spent many days and nights in the Academy as a Free Thinker. I lost track of the time as the days turned into months, and the months turned into years. Years of learning and sharing with my fellow Lifelong Students and Free Thinkers.

I felt at home in this Academy, and I didn't wish to leave. But one day, the Scholars who ran the Academy approached me and said, "It's time."

I asked them, "Time for what?"

"Time to graduate."

"Graduate?"

"It's time for you to apply the lessons you've learned here, in the real world, with real people."

"I thought this was Reality."

"It is. But just because it's your Reality doesn't mean it's everyone else's Reality. True StorySellers are able to connect with people in their Realm of Reality while remaining true to their own Realm. Only by doing this can you graduate from this Academy and become a true Scholar."

"But what if I don't want to graduate? What if I want to stay here in this Academy?"

"Then you would cease to be a StorySeller and never become a true Scholar. You would instead remain a Lifelong Student. Is that what you really want?"

I thought about it for a minute and remembered the adventures I had enjoyed on my Journey as a StorySeller. Then I remembered my tendency to imprison myself in outdated Roles instead of freeing myself from those Roles at the appropriate time. I wondered if this wasn't the appropriate time to free myself of only being a Lifelong Student. Maybe it was time to become a StorySeller once again.

So I told the Scholars that I had one condition if I were to leave this Academy. I said, "I'm a salesman like my father before me and my grandfather before him. I enjoy the life of a salesman and the glorious food and drink that goes along with it. May I have your permission to continue being a salesman even after I graduate and become a Scholar?"

They looked perplexed at my odd request. Then they replied that I could be a salesman for as long as I wanted to be, as long as I was also a salesman for them. They asked me to sell their ideas as best as I could in my travels throughout the Realms.

I replied that I'd be happy to do so on one condition. I must create my own fusion recipes as I taught their Truths. I would mix and match their teachings to fit each occasion. I would, of course, give them credit. But I would need to present their ideas in my own way.

"Fusion is popular in the modern world," I told them. "I think this idea could work." They agreed and sent me on my way.

As they did so, I learned another important lesson. Some would say it's the most important lesson of all. Without a good sales-person, no sales organization can possibly survive. And all orga-nizations are sales organizations. They sell their Stories to their Ideal Clients. Some organizations sell good Stories. Other orga-nizations, not so much.

The Scholars informed me that their organization was strug-gling with one particular demographic of their target market. They told me of the Rebels and their Battlefield. They showed me pictures of how it was littered with the dead bodies of Scholars who dared to enter. Those unfortunate Scholars had apparently tried to mediate a truce between the Rebels and the Adults. All diplomatic efforts were completely unsuccessful.

After telling me these Stories of failed attempts by others who were much smarter than me, the Scholars paused. Then they looked at me with twinkles in their eyes and dared me to take the challenge.

They said, "Your mission, should you choose to accept it, is to use the Truth you've discovered on your Journey to free the Rebels from their chains. Otherwise, you'll die on their Battlefield as a meaningless failure after living as a meaningless loser."

"That's harsh," I said.

"That's Reality," they replied.

"Whose Reality?" I asked.

"Theirs. And soon to be yours."

"What if I don't want to do it?"

"Well, Option 1 is to continue on your Journey and fulfill your next and final mission. This will tell us whether you're a true Scholar. Option 2 is to remain here in the Academy as a Lifelong Student, always wondering what would have happened if you chose Option 1."

"I see."

"You see?"

"Yes. I see and I agree. I'll do it. I'll free the Rebels from their chains."

The Scholars looked at each other. Then they looked at me. Then one of them said softly, "Christ healed the blind and raised the dead, but the Fool he could not cure."

I was later told the Voice that spoke those words belonged to the Master. On my way out of the Academy, I met the Master, who was a nearly forgotten Scholar, closely related to the Prophet.

The Master lived as a guest in the House of Reason and Knowledge, who were twin sisters. On the day of my visit, Reason and Knowledge were counting the Wise people in the Realm. The sisters were planning out their calendar for the coming week and would be visiting the Wise.

When I asked why they were counting the Wise, they replied that counting the Fools in the Realm would take too long. However, the Wise are in short supply in every Realm of Reality. Besides, even if they were able to count the Fools and pay them a visit, the effort would be futile. The Fools wouldn't open their doors. Even if the Fools did open their doors to Reason and Knowledge, they would quickly become bored with their guests and kick them out.

Then the Voice of the Master spoke to me: "Learn the words of Wisdom uttered by the Wise. Apply them in your own life.

Live them. But don't make a show of reciting them. For he who repeats what he does not understand is no better than an ass that is loaded with books."

I really should have followed his sound advice, especially when I entered the Battlefield of Rebels. Unfortunately for me, my own words would not be so masterful. In fact, they would land me in more trouble than I ever could have imagined possible.

I should have remembered that the true mission of a Scholar is to listen, not to talk. Instead, I talked without listening. I should have remembered that the best way to learn something is to teach it. Instead, I had no interest in learning. I was only interested in teaching others that which I had not yet learned myself.

Perhaps if I had avoided those blunders, I would not have found myself being led to my own death at the Altar of other people's Freedom. But alas, even the wisest Scholars make the stupidest mistakes.

CHAPTER 10

The Battlefield of Rebels

THE MISSION:

Free us from our chains...or die as a meaningless failure after living as a meaningless loser.

I DESCENDED THE MOUNTAIN OF SCHOLARS AND FOUND MYSELF on the Battlefield of Rebels. The Adults were encamped on one side of the Battlefield, and the Rebels were encamped on the other.

> The Rebels wore red, white, and blue outfits to signify their individualism.

> The Adults wore dark suits with gold ties to signify their authoritarianism.

> The Rebels carried megaphones into which they shouted incessantly.

> The Adults carried wads of cash, which they hoarded obsessively.

> The Rebels waved their hands angrily as they demanded Justice.

> The Adults folded their hands quietly as they imprisoned Justice.

> The Rebels responded furiously by shouting even louder.

> The Adults shrugged in apathy as they ate their bowls of chowder.

> The Rebels tried to get attention with shock and awe tactics.

> The Adults responded with platitudes and semantics.

The Rebels began to despair, and some started to retreat.

The Adults began to cheer, seeing the Rebels were nearly beat.

The Chief Rebel then appeared and tried to rally her people.

But the Rebels were divided into small groups of arguing people.

They wanted different things, and no one could unite them.

They longed for lots of things and couldn't decide among them.

They seemed to be tied up and bound with invisible chains.

I wondered how I could help them, as I saw their many pains.

I looked at the Adults with their dark suits and gold ties.

I felt compelled to join the Rebels and to help them rise.

I wanted them to soar like eagles and transcend their pain and misery.

I wanted them to roar like lions and remember their storied history.

They were Artists, Explorers, and Magicians, the Heroes of Humankind.

I wanted them to embrace their Destiny, but the right words escaped my mind.

I felt compelled to join the camp of the Rebels, so I did. Or at least I tried to. I approached the Rebel leader and asked to join her team. When she asked me why, I replied, "I feel your pain, and I've often wondered what I could do or what I could say to express my solidarity with your Rebel cause. And, well, here I am, ready to free you from your chains and fight with you to the death!"

Then I recited some of the wonderful words of wisdom I had learned in the Academy of Scholars. I told her all the ways that I could help her:

> I spoke my Truth to her like a Philosopher and instructed her like a learned Scholar. I said to her wise things, smart things, and true things. I lectured her in the Voice of the Master, as though I was her master.

> I quoted, "Reason is light in darkness, as anger is darkness amidst light." Then I interpreted for her like an interpreter and expounded for her like a pastor. I said, "Stop being so angry and be more reasonable like me! Your life would be way better that way, don't you see?"

> I regurgitated smart sayings, such as, "The obstacle is the way and don't let any obstacle stand in your way." I impressed myself with my witticisms and thought she'd be impressed by my criticisms.

But she wasn't. Not in the least bit.

Instead, she was completely turned off by me (I have no clue why!). She was completely unimpressed with my noble but apparently feeble attempt to help her and join her Rebel cause.

"What makes you think we want to fight to the death?" she asked me. "And what makes you think we need your help to do it?"

Good point, I thought. So I stumbled over my words a bit more and managed a feeble apology. Again, she didn't seem amused.

"Look," she said. "Only misfits are welcome here. You don't look like a misfit. You look like you belong with the Adults. You're all corporate-looking, with your business swagger, your salesman quips, and your silly quotes. You waltz onto *my* Battlefield as though you can somehow sell me something I need when what I really need is to be rid of the likes of you! Men like you have ignored us Rebels for so long, and now you come marching onto our Battlefield pretending to be one of us. Shame on you!"

The Rebels in the camp were starting to get agitated. Clearly, I was rubbing them the wrong way. They started encircling me, angrily, as though they were ready to pounce. I felt that any minute they would start beating the living shit out of me. I felt as if anything I said at this point would only serve to make the situation worse. I clearly didn't understand their language, and they didn't understand mine. *How could we possibly communicate?*

The Chief Rebel glared at me. "One last chance, dumbass. One last chance to tell us what we want to hear...what we *need* to hear in order to accept your Story."

Then she raised the stakes. "You wanna fight to the death? Fine. Go fight for the Adults. You'll die as a meaningless failure after living as a meaningless loser. But whatever you do, get the hell off my Battlefield. You don't belong here."

I looked down, visibly shaken. Why was this Rebel turning me away and pushing me back toward the Adults? I wondered what my Worthy Rival would do, and why she was nowhere to be seen. I wondered what the other Scholars would do. I imagined them jeering at me, even now, from their Ivory Towers in the Academy.

Why was I here in this Realm of Rebels all alone, competing against myself, trying to convince these people that I was on their side? I was clearly out of place here, and I seemed very much out of my element.

I thought maybe the Chief Rebel was right. Maybe I wasn't a Rebel after all. Maybe I belonged with the Adults. Maybe I would, after all my journeying and all my adventuring, die here on this Battlefield as a meaningless failure after living as a meaningless loser.

The self-doubt I felt in that moment was the strongest I had felt in all my Journey through the Realms of Reality. I needed my Story to be accepted by these Rebels or I would fail in my mission.

Most importantly, I would fail to find my UAWS. All of my adventures would have ended in vain, here among the Rebels, where I was most unwelcome.

What could I share with these Rebels to get them to understand that I was on their side? That I was one of them? That I belonged with them and not with the Adults?

I tried to think clearly, but clear thoughts evaded me. I felt in that moment only raw emotion and pure exhaustion. The type of exhaustion one would feel at the end of a long Journey through the Realms of Reality. The type of raw emotion one would feel when they find out that they're destined to be a failure after all and that victory was unattainable.

I looked at the Chief Rebel and humbly asked for a five-minute break. "Just five minutes, please, so I can gather my thoughts. Please understand." I begged, "I'm at the end of a long Journey, and I'm not quite sure where to go from here or how to tell you the Story you want to hear."

She sneered at me. "You want five minutes?"

"Yes, please."

"I'll do better than that. I'll give you twenty minutes. Meet me at the Altar of Freedom at the far side of this Battlefield in twenty minutes. Then we'll decide whether to kill you at the Altar or allow you to live. If I were a betting person, which I am, I'd bet against you every day of the week and twice on Sunday."

The Rebels laughed at her crude humor at my expense. Some even began to take bets against me. I was later told the odds reached greater than a million to one. Not a single person was willing to bet on me, and there were over a million bets against me.

I took my twenty minutes to walk around a bit and think. I recalled the lessons I had learned on my Journey so far, and how one theme seemed to repeat itself: Empathy. Whenever I was in any Realm of Reality, if I could somehow identify with the feelings of the group I was with, I could create a winning story that would appeal to them and win them over. What could be my winning story in this Realm of Rebels?

Well, I tell you, I looked carefully at the camp of the Adults and then again at the camp of the Rebels. I saw parents in both camps who were enslaved by the Disappointment and Unrealistic Expectations of their children. And then I saw children who were enslaved by the Disappointment and Unrealistic Expectations of their parents, even though they were children no more.

The Past had enslaved all those living in the Present, and it made the Future seem as grim to them as the Past. The Adults and the Rebels seemed completely at odds with each other. Yet, they were completely the same in what they wanted from one another. Each wanted freedom from the other, and understanding of their cause. Each firmly believed in their own righteousness and wanted the other to see their pain.

The Adults seemed to be winning the battle because the Rebels were scattered. In one section of the Battlefield, there were aggrieved Rebels who represented no more than 10 percent of the population. But the fascinating thing is that not too long ago, they somehow managed to acquire 100 percent of the megaphones on the Battlefield. They were called the Ten-Percenters.

The Ten-Percenters, because of their remarkable achievement in loudness, gave all the other Rebels inspiration. The other Rebels felt that they too could achieve similar results by simply acquiring louder megaphones. So that's exactly what they did. Those loud, rambunctious Rebels who first acquired louder megaphones became known as the Five-Percenters (their cause represented 5 percent of the population).

This gave even more Rebels inspiration, until eventually less than 1 percent of the population controlled 100 percent of the megaphones on the Battlefield. Those loudest of Rebels became known as the One-Percenters.

This wild turn of events made the Adults very angry. The Adults responded by creating their own privately owned economic system. They made fortunes by selling ever-louder megaphones to the Rebels! This sneaky but admittedly genius behavior resulted in 1 percent of the Adults controlling almost 100 percent of the wealth in the Realm.

Those Adults also became known as the One-Percenters. So the Adult One-Percenters with their massive Wealth battled the Rebel One-Percenters with their massive megaphones. This left the Ninety-Eight-Percenters wondering, *What the hell happened to peace and tranquility?*

The Ninety-Eight-Percenters longed for a simpler, quieter time when God was God and Man was Man and Woman put everyone in their place. It seemed simpler to them that way. They longed for the good old days, forgetting that the good old days weren't as good as they remembered. In fact, to many, the good old days were actually quite oppressive.

Even so, the Ninety-Eight-Percenters realized they were flawed people living in an imperfect world, where the best anyone can do is just do their best. But how could they possibly explain that in terms that anyone would understand? Everyone around them seemed to be making everything important except the things that were important to them.

I quickly found myself in the camp of the Ninety-Eight-Percenters who valued all the things that were no longer valued. We valued things like meaningful work and silent productivity. Things like human choice and clam chowder, lots of chowder from Boston. And lobster from Maine. And Italian pasta served with wine from Napa.

And French Armagnac that was better than cognac. American burgers served with scotch and beer. Fried fish and grilled fish. Chocolate and other candy.

And music and dancing. Lots of dancing. Salsa and samba. Tango and hip-hop. Jazz with pizzazz and good old rock and roll.

You know, all *those* types of valuable things.

I wondered why the Rebels were always so angry and why the Adults were always so solemn. I felt drawn to the Rebel cause, but I had no idea how to communicate with them.

I thought, *If only someone could unite these people, these Children of Life, and show them a better way. Perhaps they'd find a way to leave this wretched Battlefield and find a Paradise of Peace in one of the other Realms.*

172 • THE STORYSELLER ADVENTURES

I wanted to share with them how, along my Journey through the Realms, I had met all sorts of good people who were Rebels at heart. I wanted to tell them stories of how those brave human beings had created establishments in all the Realms where Rebels could live productive lives in peace.

I wanted to direct them to the Community of Friendly Neighbors and show them how to make Magic with the Magicians. I wanted them to explore the Blue Ocean of Life and race in chariots across the Arena. I wanted them to see how they could make the Imperfect Magnificent like all the great Artists who came before them.

But words escaped me, and I saw no escape from this Battlefield. In fact, as I thought about all those things, chains of Disappointment and Unrealistic Expectations began to form across my wrists. The odd thing is I didn't even realize it.

My twenty minutes was up. It was now time to meet the Chief Rebel at her Altar of Freedom, where my fate would be decided.

As I walked through the camps and toward the Altar of Freedom, a little child took my hand and smiled at me. I don't know where the little child came from or to which camp she belonged. I only noticed her delicate human touch and her beautiful human smile. I smiled back at her because in that moment, I became a little child too.

Then my smile quickly faded away as the Reality of my situation set in. As I walked toward the tragic fate that awaited me at the Altar of other people's Freedom, I couldn't help but think that this Reality was the most tragic of all the others that I had visited.

In this Realm of Rebels, all of humanity cannot help but become at once parent and child. Rebel and Adult. Oppressor and oppressed. Each in our own way dying on this Battlefield in chains of our own making while rebelling against our inevitable fate. Dying when we should be living. Fighting when we should be playing. Crying alone when we should be laughing together.

But let me tell you, these Rebels, on this Battlefield, at this moment in time, were not ready to die. They were destined to live. They were destined to achieve their victory and break free from the invisible chains of Disappointment and Unrealistic Expectations that had enslaved them for so long. These Rebels had apparently been promised a brighter future foretold to them by one whom they called the Prophet.

"The Prophet said to us that we will be free one day," one Rebel informed me as he was leading me to the Altar of Freedom, where I was to be sentenced in the name of Faith and Freedom. Whose Faith? I'm not sure. Whose Freedom? Certainly not mine. But I asked the Rebel anyway.

"You want to be free from what exactly?"

"Free from the chains that bind us, of course."

"But I see no visible chains, and you are not visibly bound. Am I missing something?" I felt as though I needed to finally get cheeky with these Rebels and challenge them.

What could I have to lose at this point? I was just going to tell them like it is. But they rebelled against my rebellion. They fought back at my defense. They asked incredulously, "How can you not see our chains?"

I struggled to explain myself. *How can I tell these people that they are already free, and that nobody is binding them in chains? How could I possibly explain to them (without getting murdered outright here and now) that they seem to be rebelling against a status quo that they've unwittingly imposed upon themselves?*

I wanted to tell them, "It's all in your head" but feared that if I did so, they'd shoot me in the head. If my goal was to win their hearts and minds, I was apparently doing a very poor job of it.

So I did what any reasonable person would do. I pulled out my calculator. One thing I forgot to mention is that a StorySeller always carries a calculator. And a spreadsheet.

As I pulled out my calculator and spreadsheet, I remembered my time back in the City of Dreams. I remembered how a professional baseball player who strikes out seven of ten times is still considered a superstar.

Then I ran the numbers. What if I ignored the One-Percenters, who weren't interested in any type of change? Nothing I could possibly say or do would convince them to give up their wealth or their megaphones. What if I ignored them and simply focused on the Ninety-Eight-Percenters?

If I could convince just 30 percent of the Ninety-Eight-Percenters to free themselves from their self-imposed chains, I would be considered a superstar in the modern world.

Perhaps I could convince a few of these Rebels to leave this Battlefield and claim their rightful place in the Realms of Reality. I switched gears and asked the Rebels another question, feeling less cheeky with each passing step toward the Altar.

"Tell me more about the Prophet you speak of. Is it a he or she? Which pronouns should I use? What's his or her Story?"

The mood lightened a bit when someone laughed at my joke. Then it got tense again when I clarified that I wasn't joking. They read too much into my meaning, when I only meant to be human. I was trying to learn more about their belief system and their Prophet so I could find some common ground. But they didn't see it that way.

We reached the Altar, across from which the Chief Rebel was sitting in her judgment seat. "The Prophet was the Prophet," the Chief Rebel barked at me as though I was a little impertinent child. "The Prophet said that one day, someone would enter our Realm and free us from our chains." She paused for effect. Then she continued, as if recounting a sacred, holy vision.

"Here at this Altar of Freedom, where Freedom is worshipped and adored, the Prophet prophesied."

The Rebels chanted in reply, "The Prophet prophesied!"

The Chief Rebel's voice started quivering, and beads of sweat began to form on her forehead. *Was she nervous?* I couldn't tell. She started shaking in her chair. *Was she having a seizure?*

Again, I couldn't tell. Then, suddenly, her shaking stopped and she continued, her voice still quivering:

"The Prophet prophesied."

The Rebels chanted back, "The Prophet prophesied!"

Then silence. Total silence. I was totally confused. So I asked another question:

"Okay, and then what happened?"

The Chief Rebel stared at me. The others did too. I met her gaze and stared right back. *First person to talk loses!* She lost.

"What do you mean 'and then what happened?'"

"You said the Prophet prophesied."

"Yes."

"Well, what did the Prophet prophesy?"

Her eyebrows furrowed like a maniac, and she looked pissed.

"I've already told you... The prophet prophesied that we would be free from our chains!"

My line of questioning clearly wasn't working. This conversation was going nowhere. I stupidly asked another question, trying to stall the inevitable judgment headed my way. "Did the Prophet say *how* you would be freed from your chains?"

The Chief Rebel glared at me, eyes bulging out of their sockets, and then she screamed her final high-pitched reply, "I've already *told* you! The Prophet said that one day someone would enter our Realm and free us from our chains!"

I got the hint that maybe I was pushing too far, so I took a step back. And as I did, I mistakenly bumped into the Altar. The Rebels gasped. I clumsily apologized and tried to change the subject. "Fine. Okay then. Thanks for your patience in explaining that all to me. I totally get it."

I tried to summarize what I had just heard, hoping that I could stall my impending death with some clever words, or maybe even a Story. Then it dawned on me.

Had the same Voice that called to me that day long ago also called upon them? Perhaps the Voice was their Prophet. After all, the Voice promised me that I too would be free if I embarked on this Journey through the Realms of Reality.

I asked the Rebels, "Did you ever meet the Prophet face-to-face, or was it a Voice that spoke to you here, at your Altar of Freedom?"

They seemed to be taken aback by my question. The Chief Rebel perked up in her seat as she answered, "It was a Voice. How do you know that? Do you know the Prophet who prophesied here at this Altar?"

I replied cautiously, carefully choosing my words, hoping that I was onto something, "I met a 'Prophet' once too, you see. The Prophet told me that all the knowledge I have is in vain and worthless unless I work hard to apply that knowledge.

"All the hard work I do to apply my knowledge is completely useless unless I do my work with love. When I do my work with love, I'll find my truest self. I'll connect with others and become one with God himself.

"Only then will I find my Unique, Authentic Winning Self and free myself from my own chains of Disappointment and Unrealistic Expectations. Did your Prophet ever say anything like that to you?"

A quiet stillness descended upon the group. The Chief Rebel motioned for me to continue. I continued recounting my own Story, with a few embellishments, of course.

"I was enslaved once, just like you. And my chains were like yours. They prevented me from being free. The Prophet told me that I can be free when I rise above my sorrow and worries as though I am free because, in reality, I was born free.

"I was born completely naked, after all, with nothing hindering me! The only expectation I had at that time was that everything would somehow be okay. I was born free from any of the worries that bind me now.

"The Prophet told me to become like that child again. He said that my childlike self would grow wings like those of an angel. Then I could use those angelic wings to fly out of the cage that I had unwittingly built to enslave myself.

"So I did just that. I became like a little child and grew some wings. Then I went on a little adventure, except my little adventure turned out to be not so little after all!

"It was actually a glorious, larger-than-life adventure. It was a thrilling adventure where I battled Shape-Shifters and Evil Sorcerers and raced in my chariot around the Arena. It was an exquisite culinary adventure where I ate and drank with Friendly Neighbors and Outsiders—all in the same place, no less!

"It was an adventure where I laughed with Comedians, cried with Artists, and marveled at the simultaneous beauty and ugliness of Life. It was an adventure where I fought alongside the bravest Warriors and ruled with the wisest Rulers and studied at the feet of the smartest Scholars. It was an adventure that led me here to you, the Rebels, the ones who are destined to be free."

The silence among the group was deafening. I couldn't tell what the Rebels were thinking or how they were going to react to my Story. Then someone I couldn't see whispered softly, "Are you the One?"

I asked the unseen Rebel to repeat the question.

"Are you the *One*, the Prophet foretold would free us from our chains?"

"No, of course not. Of course I'm not the One. I...I..."

"Then who are you?"

"Well, I'm a...I'm a...I'm a StorySeller."

"A StorySeller?"

"Yes."

"What's that?"

"Well, as best as I can tell, it's a human being like us who sells Rebels like us a story of how we can become the best version of ourselves and free ourselves from the chains that bind us to the lesser versions of ourselves."

"Hmm. Interesting. So you're really a Rebel?"

"I suppose I am."

"But I thought you said you were a StorySeller."

"Well, I'm that too!"

"How can you be more than one thing?"

"Here's the thing, my friends. I don't really know *how*. All I know is that if someone were to tell you that *you* can only be one thing, that would be sort of like imposing an arbitrary rule on you, correct? And Rebels like us, we don't like arbitrary rules. In fact, we rebel against them. That's why we're called Rebels. So of course we can be more than one thing. At least, it seems that way to me. What do you think?"

The Rebels looked around at each other for validation, but they seemed to be, for the most part, in agreement with my reasoning, which, I must confess, was quite sound and worthy of agreement. *Why wouldn't everyone agree with me all the time, after all?*

I sighed in relief as it dawned on me that I may have averted my own death with my little Story. Naturally, I felt like patting myself on the back, but regrettably, I couldn't. Just as I was feeling intense pride at the Altar of Freedom, the Chief Rebel rose from her seat and rushed at me with such urgency that it startled me.

I had no idea what this crazy person had in mind or what she would do next. I had no clue at all why she was rushing at me so furiously like a demon out of hell. My heart skipped a beat with each hurried step that she took as she approached me.

"You *are* the One!" she exclaimed as she enveloped me with a gigantic bear hug. "You're the one the Prophet foretold would rescue us from the Adults and free us from our chains. Why should we sacrifice our better selves here at the Altar of our own Freedom when we can journey with you through the Realms of Reality?"

"But, I..."

"No buts or I's. It's only we's and us's from here on out. Let's do this thing! Let's break free and join the adventure!"

Then she turned to the Rebels, and they roared in agreement. Their howling grew and grew and grew until the crowd was standing in ovation for the great orator before them. Or maybe not.

I wasn't quite sure whether they were applauding my haphazard speech or cheering the Freedom that I had promised to them. Either way, I joined them in their applause. In fact, I was very happy to do so, if for no other reason than my realization that, once again, I had somehow managed to join a group of people who seemed to be sort of like me.

We were fellow Rebels choosing to free ourselves from the invisible chains that bound us to lesser versions of our truest selves.

One by one, we approached the Altar. And one by one, we realized our chains weren't real. When it was my turn, I laid down all of my brokenness on the Altar of my own Freedom. Then I climbed on the Altar and sacrificed my lesser self, knowing that I would somehow be resurrected like so many Rebels who had taken this Journey before me.

Little did I know that our newfound Freedom and resurrection would carry with it a cost. A cost that would destroy the fortunes of some and bring newfound fortune to others. A cost that would be paid for with our blood, tears, and sweat...again and again and again, from now until the end of our days. A cost that was paid by all those who came before us and will undoubtedly be paid by all those who come after us.

Our Freedom, won here at this Altar, would come at an immeasurable cost that reminds us time after time what it means to be immeasurably human.

Yet, in spite of the cost imposed by our humanity, ushered in by our Freedom, and paid for with our blood, we rebelled. We broke free. We set aside our invisible chains of Disappointment that had enslaved us for so long, and we freed ourselves on the Altar of our own Freedom.

After letting go of our chains of Disappointment and Unrealistic Expectations, we soared on the wings of angels until the wings of our better angels brought us to the Hall of Mirrors, where our final fate would be decided.

Little did I realize whom I would meet or what he would tell me. Or how I'd object and how he'd compel me.

CHAPTER 11

The Hall of Mirrors

AFTER LOSING MYSELF IN THE REALMS OF REALITY, I FOUND myself in the Hall of Mirrors, face-to-face with my own humanity.

The Hall was filled with Mirrors of Life reflecting back at me the places, characters, and sights from my Journey. It was as if I was watching the movie of my life playing right before my eyes. I saw myself winning sales and losing sales, entertaining clients and being entertained by them.

Then the Mirrors of Life shifted, and I saw my father on his Journey and my grandfather before him on his. I observed my father winning sales and losing sales and my grandfather entertaining clients and being entertained by them. I noticed that the characters and places on their Journeys were quite different from the ones I encountered on mine. Yet, they were somehow very much the same.

The Mirrors of Life shifted again, and I saw my clients on their Journey, and my Worthy Rival on hers. I saw my friends, my colleagues, and all my relatives. I gazed at the images of everyone I had ever known reflected back at me in the Mirrors, and it was as if I was seeing them all for the first time.

The Mirrors of Life shifted one last time, and I saw all of humanity from the beginning of time until now. The heroes and villains of antiquity came to life for me, along with the gods and goddesses who challenged and empowered them on their Journeys. Their Stories blended with mine, and I began to see my own chapter in the epic story of humanity. I became one with humankind and yet somehow one with myself.

Then the Mirrors of Life began to dance with one another, embracing each other and then separating again, and then blending together until there was only one mirror left. I looked a little closer into that one dancing mirror and saw in it the reflection of God himself.

It was about that time that the Voice spoke to me once again. It seemed more scholarly and mature as it instructed me, "Even as you were created in the image of your Creator, your creations, products, and services are created in your own image. They reflect the Warrior, Explorer, Magician, Ruler, Comedian, Friend, Artist, Scholar, and Rebel inside of you. Step 1 to discovering and living your Unique, Authentic Winning Story is to pick your primary archetype and where you are in your Journey at this moment. Step 2 is to communicate with others in a language they can understand based on their primary archetype and where they are in their Journey at this moment.

"One of the Realms will speak to you more than the others. It's the Realm into which you were born. The Optimists were right.

You were born in the Realm of Reality where your heart sings for joy and everything else just fades away or dissolves into the background.

"Your clients, your coworkers, and your family and friends are all the same way. One of the Realms speaks to them more than the others because it's the Realm into which they were born. That's where their heart sings for joy and everything else just fades away or dissolves into the background.

"A true StorySeller finds a way to bridge the gap between the two Realms—between the two Stories.

"The Ruler in you can speak peacefully with the Rebel in a language the Rebel understands. Thus, you can create a Paradise of Peace in any Realm that is filled with Chaos.

"The Warrior in you can strengthen the hand of the Artist as she transforms the Imperfect into the Magnificent, while the Magician helps the Explorer find hidden Treasures scattered across the Blue Ocean of Life. The Scholar can illuminate the Truth, while the Comedian lightens the many burdens of the Friendly Neighbor.

"As for the Rebel, the Rebel inside of you can free you and your fellow travelers from chains of your own making and liberate you at the Altar of your own Freedom as the Prophet prophesied."

I thought of those words and meditated on them for what seemed like an eternity. Then I remembered myself. I remembered myself as a child, as a youth, and as an Adult. Yes, I'm ashamed to say that I was an Adult once. But that's another story for another time.

"You're right," I said to the Voice. "I had it both right and wrong all along."

"I'm glad you see that now," the Voice replied. Then we had the most unexpected, peculiar conversation I think I've ever had. It all started with one very invasive, completely not right, ridiculous question. The Voice asked me about my religion (gasp!). He looked at me in front of God and everybody and asked, "What religion are you?"

"Excuse me?"

"What's your religion?"

I replied by asking what difference my religion made to him or anyone else. He replied that one's religion was "the eyes through which you see your Story." Then he said, "Some have blue eyes and some have brown. Some see through green eyes and others are blind in their eyes of religion but see their Story through the divine eyes of the humanity within them."

I replied that my eyes were brown and that I am a student of all religions because I am a firm believer in my own.

"Very good," he said. "It's very good that you know your religion and that you're okay with it. Some people are afraid or ashamed of their religion, and thus afraid or ashamed of their own Story. They close their eyes when they should be open. But that, in itself, is a story for another time."

Then he asked me another very invasive, completely not right, ridiculous question. He asked whether I was a liberal or a conservative. *The gall of this guy!* I replied that I was a conservative liberal and a liberal conservative. I seek to conserve the beliefs I hold sacred on my Journey while liberating others to do the same on their Journey.

He acknowledged my answer and warned that the world in which I live may at some point (if it hasn't already) try to use my religious and political beliefs against me. "They'll 'cancel' you at the first whiff that you're not like them," he cautioned.

"They'll try to shackle you with their chains of Disappointment and Unrealistic Expectations in the name of Faith and Freedom. In those moments, and in every moment, stay true to yourself.

Gaze into the Mirrors of Life and see that you and your fellow travelers are Children of Life together. May your life's work and your life's story be your love letter to humanity and your offering to your God. Expect nothing from the world in return and receive blessings from your God at every turn."

I nodded slowly and asked whether I could be so bold as to ask him a very invasive, completely not right, ridiculous question. After all, it seemed only fair that I should be able to do so now that we were becoming so well acquainted. He seemed amused at my impertinence and gave his assent.

I asked him in front of God and everybody, "Why must you talk with such lofty words and lyrical phrases? Why must you communicate with me in allegories and analogies and all sorts of metaphors that make you seem smart, stupid, and pretentious all at the same time?"

I paused for effect, trying to rattle him, but he didn't seem rattled. His silence seemed to egg me on. So I continued mockingly, "You're constantly like, 'There is this and there is that, and that becomes this and this becomes that, and all the world is like a song and all the songs are like the world... Blah, blah, blah.' It's actually quite annoying, you know. The way you talk is ridiculous! It's like you're singing a song but telling a story but teaching a lesson all at the same time. It's so freaking weird!"

"Ah, yes, I know," he chuckled.

"But why? Why do you do it?"

"I guess that's the way I think, the way I communicate when I have something important to say."

"But why? Why are you like that?"

"I'm not sure exactly. Maybe it's the double meanings of the words and phrases in the songs I listened to as a child. Maybe it's the rhythm of the nursery rhymes that constantly play in my head as I raise my own children. Or perhaps it's the inner child in me that comes out when I write like this. Maybe it's the scriptures I memorized when I was younger, or the hymns I sang in my youth, or the poems that inspire me when I'm most in need of inspiration.

"But here's a clever idea I've got for you. I know what we can do!

"I'll sell you my Story in the way I sell it and you sell me your Story in the way you sell it! I'll be me and you be you. Does that sound good to you?"

"There you go again! It's like you're singing a song without actually singing a song! Stop it!"

"I can't stop it. It's like asking a Warrior to stop fighting or a Ruler to stop ruling."

"Stop it!"

"I can't stop it. It's like asking a Comedian to stop laughing or an Artist to stop creating."

"Stop it!"

"I can't stop it. It's like asking an Explorer to stop exploring or a Scholar to stop studying."

"Stop it! Stop it, I say!"

"I can't. Never. No way! It's like asking a Friendly Neighbor to be an Outsider or a Magician to cease from performing magic."

"That's quite enough!"

"You're right! It is quite enough to be yourself—to soar on the wings of your better angels, to sing the melodies of your heart, and to dance to those melodies here in the Hall of Mirrors with all of humanity watching.

"I've learned how some people in your world tik and tok, and others talk with tics, and yet others simply walk their walk. But verily, verily I say unto you, I must simply talk like I talk and walk like I walk! You must be you and I must be me. That's the idea, don't you *see*?"

How exasperating! How exhausting! I just could not find the strength within me to argue with this crazy Voice any longer. So, my friend, I finally gave in to the Voice of my future self in the Hall of Mirrors, in front of God and everybody.

And so it came to pass that at the end of a long Journey, probably not all that different from your own, I found my Unique, Authentic Winning Story by finding my Unique, Authentic Winning Self.

As for those pesky questions I had in the beginning of my Journey when I first followed the Voice—those ridiculous questions about whether I mattered, whether I'd make a difference, and how I could make money—remember *those* questions?

Well, I learned that the nearness of the answers to Life's questions often depends on how far one is willing to travel to find them. And, of course, whether one's eyes are open while traveling. In my case, my answers turned out to be closer to me than I had imagined. I needed only to open my eyes and see the surprises that were in store for me.

For instance, I learned that in order to *matter to others*, I must *matter to myself*. I must care enough about others and myself to become the best version of myself. I must sacrifice any and all lesser versions on the Altar of my own Freedom, leaving my invisible chains of Disappointment and Unrealistic Expectations behind.

I learned that in order to *make a difference,* I need to *be different.* In order to *avoid insignificance,* I need to create *significant value.* I learned that any value I create is meaningless unless it's simple for others to understand in their own language, on their own Journey, and in their own Realm of Reality.

And yes, I also learned how to *make money* by applying these lessons in my day-to-day work. I'll share with you some of those lessons in Part II of this book.

The most important lessons I learned, however, were the ones I learned about how to find myself after losing myself, and how to make my way back to this sacred Hall of Mirrors whenever I lose my way. I learned how to not lose at life, regardless of whether I win or lose in business. I learned all these things on my Journey through the Realms of Reality, and more—much, much more. I can't wait to tell you more about those things in the next two books of this adventure!

As for the Adults? Of course, they tried to stop me and my fellow StorySellers from being ourselves and selling our Stories. Here, in this sacred Hall of Mirrors, in front of God and everybody, they shamelessly turned the Rebels among us against the Rulers, and the Rulers among us against the Rebels.

They stirred up ungodly amounts of Fear and Sectarianism in the Community of Friendly Neighbors and created mountains of Useless Data to confuse the Scholars. They took advantage of the worst sensibilities of the Comedians and played parlor tricks on the Magicians.

They shipwrecked the Explorers and "canceled" the Warriors. They turned winners into losers and made losers their leaders. They destroyed the magnificence of humanity with grotesque amounts of Perfectionism and Mediocrity. They chiseled away at the Magnificent until it became the Imperfect.

They turned our religions against us and closed our eyes to so many beautiful viewpoints that we could have enjoyed by simply traveling with our eyes open. They wielded the weapons of conservatism and liberalism to illiberally destroy the way of life we wanted to conserve.

They created algorithms to divide us, and they mercilessly chopped us into fractions of ourselves. They transformed many of us into burned-out losers instead of helping all of us become the triumphant winners that we were born to be. All this they did, and more—much, much more. But that, my friend, is another story for another time.

As for this story, it seems as though it's time to come to the end of this chapter of our not-so-little adventure. One cannot gaze into the Mirrors of Life and talk to oneself forever or else boredom will turn our self-love into self-loathing and, well, you know the rest (sigh).

Just as I was gathering my wits about me, the Voice spoke up again and asked me a question that I'll never forget: "What's next for you?"

"What's next for *me*?"

"Yes, *you*."

"Well, I suppose I'll go back to being a traveling salesman, like my grandfather before me. It's in our blood, you know. Sales. It's truly the greatest profession in the world! I'll schedule a business trip through the Realms of Reality as a traveling Story-Seller. I'll help my fellow travelers in each Realm discover and live their Unique, Authentic Winning Story (UAWS for short)."

"Sounds like a plan."

"Let's do this thing!"

Just like that, I decided to go in another direction. I'm sure you understand.

But wait, there's more! I hear something in the background. It's getting louder and louder with each passing second. The phone is ringing again. Only this time, if I'm not mistaken (which I don't think I am), I believe it's your phone that's ringing. It seems like the Voice, your Voice, is calling you.

Will you answer the call?

PART II

Step-by-Step Guide to the Archetypes

CHAPTER 12

The Warrior Archetype

Have you ever found yourself fighting a losing battle?

I HAVE, MANY TIMES! ONE THING I'VE FOUND USEFUL WHEN I'M fighting a losing battle is to just stop fighting for a moment and think. I try to think about why I'm losing the battle and whether it makes sense for me to continue fighting in the first place.

I was at a crossroads in my business recently after having invested lots of time and money to create and market a product that didn't turn out to be profitable. I was really invested in this product, and I really believed it was a brilliant idea! But the market didn't seem to agree with me. I wasn't gaining traction.

Then I stopped fighting for a bit and asked myself a simple question: am I fighting the right battle?

I wondered how my business would be impacted if I shifted my focus and invested the same amount of time and energy elsewhere. I realized that if I disengaged from my current losing battle, I would free up a ridiculous amount of time and energy. I could then take that time and energy and use it to fight new battles I could actually win.

In short, I channeled my inner Warrior to "sell myself a story" of how I could become a better version of myself and fight winning battles instead of losing battles.

That's how I used the Warrior archetype in my business recently. How are you using it?

Characteristics of the Warrior Archetype

- Values victory, mastery, and achievement

- Hard to win over initially, but super loyal once on the team

- Supercompetitive and focused on winning

- Fears weakness and vulnerability, respects courage

- Strong desire to make a difference and achieve significance

- Tends to become arrogant or paranoid about seeing enemies everywhere

Alternative Names for the Warrior Archetype

- Hero, Champion, Fighter

Sample Warrior Brands in Popular Culture

- Brands with a sports or victory focus

- Nike, Gatorade

Sample Warrior Archetypes in Popular Stories, Movies, and TV Shows

- Ned Stark and Jon Snow, *Game of Thrones*

- Wonder Woman and other Warrior-type superheroes

- William Wallace, *Braveheart*

- Maximus, *Gladiator*

- Winston Churchill, *The Darkest Hour*

- Rocky Balboa, *Rocky*

TOPIC	COACHING TIPS

Your Story: how to use the Warrior archetype to build your personal brand	A Warrior brand is focused on helping its clients or strategic partners win a competition or a battle. It's achievement focused, it's competitive, and it values victory.
	
	 Here are three tips you can use if you're trying to build a personal brand based on the Warrior archetype:
	
	 • When working with clients and strategic partners, focus on how you can help them win. Ask questions like:
	
	    • "What does winning look like for you?"
	
	    • "What are you trying to achieve?"
	
	    • "What are your goals?"
	
	 • Use sports metaphors, analogies, and illustrations in your marketing.
	
	 • Position your services as the ultimate "magic weapon" or "performance tool" that helps clients and strategic partners win. For example:
	
	    • "Get X result with our XYZ program."
	
	    • "Achieve X goal by working with me."

Your Client's Story: how to use the Warrior archetype to overcome objections	Warrior clients feel as if they're in a competition or a battle with you. Their initial bias is to be combative, and they are often resistant to your price or advice. StorySelling Steps: • **Step 1:** Recognize and empower the Warrior archetype. That's the mode or mental state that the client is in right now. • **Step 2:** Acknowledge that their fight is real and illustrate the specific challenge that's standing in their way. Position the market or the challenge as the villain in their story. • **Step 3:** Illustrate how your products and services are like "magic weapons" that will help the client defeat the villain, win their battle, and achieve victory. Your mission is to show them that you're in the trenches, fighting the good fight with them or on their behalf. StorySelling Tips to Overcome Objections with Clients or Strategic Partners Who Fit the Warrior Archetype: • **Lowest Cost Script:** "Do you want the lowest price or the lowest overall cost? Here's how you can save money (and headaches) by working with me..." • **Acknowledge the Fight Script:** "I understand why you would feel that way. It must be exhausting trying to __. Have you tried __? Here's how I can help..." • **Help Me Understand Script:** "Could you help me understand what you meant when you said, __?"

TOPIC	COACHING TIPS
The Market's Story: how to use the Warrior archetype to tell the story of today's market and illustrate your unique value	Here are two tips you can use if you're trying to tell the story of today's market and illustrate your unique value using the Warrior archetype: • **Today's market is like a battlefield**, and my role is to help you win the battle. • **Today's market is like an Olympic competition**, where every second matters and all your competitors are superstar athletes. My role is to help you win the competition.
Your Sales Process: how to use the Warrior archetype to save time, be more productive, and improve your sales results	Here are two tips you can use to save time and improve your sales process with the Warrior archetype: • Set numbers-based goals for yourself: "I'm going to time-block X minutes/day to knock out X sales calls." • Label time blocks in your calendar using battle or sports themes (in the trenches, daily sales workouts, etc.).
Your Strategy: how to put on your Warrior glasses and trigger profitable shifts in your business strategy	**Imagine yourself fighting a battle, and ask yourself these questions:** • Am I fighting the right battle? • What would happen if I stopped fighting this particular battle? **Imagine yourself playing a "game of business," and ask yourself these questions:** • Which game of business am I really playing? • How do I play the game that I can win? **Book Recommendations:** • *Playing to Win* • *Finite and Infinite Games* • *The Infinite Game* • *Shoe Dog*

Visit TheStorySeller.com and see *The StorySeller* podcast Episode 6 for more details.

CHAPTER 13

The Explorer Archetype

Have you ever been stranded in a place you don't want to be anymore?

THERE WAS A TIME IN MY YOUNGER DAYS WHEN I WOULD make it to the airport just in time for my flight. My colleagues would make fun of me because I was never early, but always "just in time." I was okay with this approach until one day I missed my flight! I literally got stuck in a place I didn't want to be anymore.

Nowadays, I like to go to the airport early because I understand the cost of *not* getting there early. I've found that the same principle applies in business. If I don't plan ahead, I'm taking on the risk of getting stuck somewhere in my business or career that I just don't want to be anymore. I try to channel my inner Explorer and make sure I ask myself questions like these:

- What's my destination?

- Is this the right destination?

- Do I have the right vehicles and team in place to get there, etc.?

That's how I've used the Explorer archetype in my business recently. How are you using it?

Characteristics of the Explorer Archetype

- Values unique and interesting experiences

- Very independent and doesn't like boundaries

- Likes to try new things and fears being trapped

- Seeks to express individuality

- Tends to aimlessly wander

Alternative Names for the Explorer Archetype

- Adventurer, Pioneer, Traveler, Pilgrim

Sample Explorer Brands in Popular Culture

- Experience-focused brands

- Four Seasons, Virgin, Amazon

Sample Explorer Archetypes in Popular Stories, Movies, and TV Shows

- Arya Stark, *Game of Thrones*

- Simba, *The Lion King*

- Odysseus, *The Odyssey*

TOPIC	COACHING TIPS
Your Story: how to use the Explorer archetype to build your personal brand	An Explorer brand is focused on helping its clients or strategic partners enjoy their experience and successfully get to their destination. Here are three tips you can use if you're trying to build a personal brand based on the Explorer archetype: • When working with clients and strategic referral partners, focus on how you provide an enjoyable experience and successfully get them to their destination. • If you're trying to build a luxury brand, focus on how you provide an exclusive, custom-tailored experience. • If you're trying to build an economy brand, focus on how you provide a cheaper, faster experience.
Your Client's Story: how to use the Explorer archetype to overcome objections	An Explorer client is looking for an easier, more enjoyable way to get to their destination. They don't want to be locked down just yet, and they're "just looking." StorySelling Steps: • **Step 1**: Recognize and accompany the Explorer archetype. That's the mode or mental state that the client is in right now. • **Step 2**: Illustrate the specific roadblocks that may prevent them from getting to where they want to go. You can illustrate how not working with you may get them "stuck" in a place they don't want to be. • **Step 3**: Illustrate how your services are like "special passports" that help the client enjoy their journey and get to where they want to go. StorySelling Tips to Overcome Objections with Clients or Strategic Partners Who Fit the Explorer Archetype: • **I'm just looking:** "Seems like you're just shopping around, and that's totally okay. Would you like me to put together some options for you?" • **Your price seems high, and I'm not sure I want to pay what you're asking:** "Well, it seems to me as though you want to stay at the Four Seasons and pay Holiday Inn prices. Am I missing something?" • **I'm just considering my options at this point:** "Great, which options are you considering?"
The Market's Story: how to use the Explorer archetype to tell the story of today's market and illustrate your unique value	Here are two tips you can use if you're trying to tell the story of today's market and illustrate your unique value using the Explorer archetype: • Discuss the "pitfalls" of the "wild" market and how you can help the client navigate the market and avoid the pitfalls: "Here are the top three pitfalls we're seeing right now for clients in your situation." • Discuss how the wrong strategy or working with the wrong person could cause clients or strategic partners to get "stuck" in an undesirable situation: "Today's market is like traveling out of the country in the middle of a pandemic. I just don't want you to get stuck or trapped in X situation with no way out."

TOPIC	COACHING TIPS
Your Sales Process: how to use the Explorer archetype to save time, be more productive, and improve your sales results	Here are three tips you can use to save time and improve your sales process with the Explorer archetype: • Set experience-based goals for your business: "I'm going to provide a customer experience that looks/feels like this." • Label the stages in your customer experience with fun and exciting names ("Phase 1 is shopping, Phase 2 is taking it for a test drive, etc."). • Try to find out which options your clients are currently considering. Then try to shift their focus toward the options you provide as a better way to get what they want. Don't just give them one option; give them two or three. This way they compare you versus you instead of you versus your competition.
Your Strategy: how to pull out your Explorer passport and trigger profitable shifts in your business strategy	**Imagine yourself as a great Explorer, and ask yourself these questions:** • What's my destination? • Is this the right destination? • Do I have the right vehicles and team in place to get there? **Book Recommendations:** • *Blue Ocean Strategy* • *Start with No* • *Never Split the Difference*

Visit TheStorySeller.com and see *The StorySeller* podcast Episode 7 for more details.

CHAPTER 14

The Magician Archetype

Have you ever felt as if people expected you to wave a magic wand and make all their problems disappear?

ONE OF THE BIGGEST CHALLENGES I'VE FACED IN MY OWN life and career is coming to terms with the fact that I'm just a human being and I don't have a magic wand that can just make problems go away.

It's hard enough sometimes to convince myself of that reality, but how do I convince others of that reality when they're expecting something of me that I just can't possibly deliver?

I've found that it's useful in situations like that to pull back the curtain and give the other person a glimpse of what it would take in the real world to give them what they want. I need to show them the details behind the magic trick that they're expecting me to pull off.

When I do that, it exposes the fact that I'm only human after all, and it removes the illusion that I can magically and immediately solve their problem without any effort on their part.

When I put on my Magician hat and show them how the trick works, it's much more effective than trying to perform the trick while they're still in the dark. That's because they begin to appreciate the hard work and skill it will take to get them what they're asking for. I've found it to be less stressful to enlist others in performing the magic with me, instead of thinking (naively) that I can make the magic happen all on my own.

That's how I've used the Magician archetype in my business recently. How are you using it?

Characteristics of the Magician Archetype

- Values magical moments and likes to make dreams come true for others

- Methodical, detail oriented, well researched, and thorough

- Likes to find clues and insights that are elusive or not easy to discover

- Seeks to use his or her special insights to creatively solve problems

- Fears unanticipated negative consequences or being manipulated

- Tends to get sidetracked or lost in the details

Alternative Names for the Magician Archetype

- Wizard, Fixer, Problem Solver, Dream Maker, Engineer

Sample Magician Brands in Popular Culture

- Consumer brands focused on making dreams come true

- Disney, Google, Tesla

Sample Magician Archetypes in Popular Stories, Movies, and TV Shows

- Doug Stamper, *House of Cards*

- Tom Hagen, *The Godfather*

- Gandalf, *The Lord of the Rings*

- Q, *James Bond*

TOPIC	COACHING TIPS
Your Story: how to use the Magician archetype to build your personal brand	A Magician brand is focused on skillfully or creatively helping its clients or strategic partners make their dreams come true or achieve results that may appear to be "magical" to the uninitiated.
	Here are three tips you can use if you're trying to build a personal brand based on the Magician archetype:
	• When working with clients and strategic referral partners, focus on how you have the unique ability to give them secrets, clues, and insights that are not readily available through other "normal" sources.
	• Use magical-moment-type phrases, metaphors, analogies, and illustrations in your marketing. For example, use testimonials of clients who didn't think they could ever buy a home, but you made their dream come true.
	• Position your services as "keys" that help clients and strategic partners unlock the not-so-easily-achievable results they're looking for.
Your Client's Story: how to use the Magician archetype to overcome objections	The Magician client is observant, detail oriented, well researched, methodical, and thorough. They want a behind-the-scenes peek into how things work, and they can sometimes annoy you with all their questions.
	StorySelling Steps:
	• **Step 1:** Recognize and applaud the Magician archetype. That's the mode or mental state that the client is in right now.
	• **Step 2:** Outline the specific steps required to create the "magic" they seek. Set expectations that the magic isn't as simple as it seems.
	• **Step 3:** Illustrate how your products and services are like "magic formulas" that can help the client create success.
	StorySelling Tips to Overcome Objections with Clients or Strategic Partners Who Fit the Magician Archetype:
	• Have pamphlets, detailed outlines, and templates available to answer common questions.
	• Give your strategic partners regular status updates on all the deals you have in process with them to preemptively address their questions and empower them to do their "magic."
The Market's Story: how to use the Magician archetype to tell the story of today's market and illustrate your unique value	Here are two tips you can use if you're trying to tell the story of today's market and illustrate your unique value using the Magician archetype:
	• With Clients: "Have you ever seen a magic trick and wondered how it works? Buying a home in today's market is kind of like pulling off a complicated magic trick. Here are the step-by-step details for how it works."
	• With Strategic Partners: "Your competitors have all these cool technologies they're using to dazzle the customer and steal their attention. Here's how we can work together to create some magic of our own and capture the business."

TOPIC	COACHING TIPS
Your Sales Process: how to use the Magician archetype to save time, be more productive, and improve your sales results	Here's a way to save time and improve your sales process with the Magician archetype: • Set aside time in your calendar for problem-solving difficult scenarios. This way, you establish boundaries and prevent the problem situations from taking over your life and calendar. You can label this time as "Magician time" or "problem-solving time" because that's the time you've set aside to put on your Magician hat and make your magic happen!
Your Strategy: how to put on your Magician hat and trigger profitable shifts in your business strategy	**Imagine yourself as a Master Magician, and ask yourself these questions:** • What are the specific steps to performing the magic trick I'm being asked to perform? • How can I delegate to others some of those steps or otherwise get them to do things to make the magic easier to perform? • How can I set expectations that the magic isn't as easy and as simple as it looks? **Book Recommendations:** • *Zero to One* • *Fascinate* and *How the World Sees You* • *Building a StoryBrand*

Visit TheStorySeller.com and see *The StorySeller* podcast Episode 8 for more details.

CHAPTER 15

The Ruler Archetype

Have you ever felt things spinning out of your control so quickly that your world started rocking out of balance?

THERE WAS A SITUATION IN MY BUSINESS RECENTLY THAT WAS frustrating me because no matter how hard I tried to get this thing off my plate, it lingered. The longer it lingered, the more frustrated I became. I just couldn't find a way to get it under control. Then one day, I took some time to really think about why this thing kept lingering. What was the root cause?

I realized the root cause itself was not under my control. It wasn't even under my team's control. In fact, I realized the root cause of the Chaos was actually a new normal in my world that would likely linger for a while. So I had three choices:

- Option 1: Pretend that this thing would somehow miraculously go away and "escape" every time it flares up, leaving others on my team to deal with the Chaos.

- Option 2: Pretend I have control over the situation and continue to be frustrated each time I realize I don't.

- Option 3: Give up the control I seek. Instead, create systems in my business to isolate and handle the Chaos that this thing creates whenever it flares up.

I chose Option 3. But in order to make it work, I made a decision to schedule time in my calendar to deal responsibly with the Chaos this situation creates. I'm not sure how long the root cause of the Chaos will persist, but at least I'm not allowing it to rule my life and business. By acknowledging the root cause is out of my control and setting boundaries on the Chaos it creates, I got back control of the rest of my day and became a Ruler of my little kingdom once again.

That's how I've used the Ruler archetype in my business recently. How are you using it?

Characteristics of the Ruler Archetype

- Values results, control, and strong leadership

- Focused on the big picture and gets frustrated with details

- Likes to bring order, harmony, and prosperity to his or her world

- Fears chaos, failure, or loss of control

- Looking for a clear path forward

Alternative Names for the Ruler Archetype

- King, Queen, CEO, Executive, Boss

Sample Ruler Brands in Popular Culture

- Brands focused on serving busy executives

- The Capital Grille, Amex, JPMorgan Chase, Costco

Sample Ruler Archetypes in Popular Stories, Movies, and TV Shows

- President Josiah Bartlet, *The West Wing*

- Daenerys Targaryen and Cersei Lannister, *Game of Thrones*

- Don Corleone (Vito and Michael), *The Godfather*

TOPIC	COACHING TIPS
Your Story: how to use the Ruler archetype to build your personal brand	A Ruler brand is focused on helping clients bring order, harmony, and prosperity to their sometimes-chaotic world. Here are three tips you can use if you're trying to build a personal brand based on the Ruler archetype: • When working with clients and strategic referral partners, focus on how you can safely help them achieve specific results at a fair price. • Use old-school, simple illustrations in your marketing. Don't try to be fancy or clever. • Position your services as safe, trustworthy, and proven to generate the specific results your ideal clients and referral partners are looking for.
Your Client's Story: how to use the Ruler archetype to overcome objections	A Ruler client is super busy and just looking for bottom-line results. No hype, no bells and whistles, no fancy-schmancy gimmicks. Just quick, bottom-line results. Period. StorySelling Steps: • **Step 1:** Recognize and respect the Ruler archetype. That's the mode or mental state that the client is in right now. • **Step 2:** Illustrate the various instances of chaos invading their realm. This demonstrates a clear grasp of their executive-level challenges. • **Step 3:** Illustrate how your products and services can help them "tame the chaos" and bring order back to their world. StorySelling Tips to Overcome Objections with Clients or Strategic Partners Who Fit the Ruler Archetype: • Communicate in bullet points. • Give clients and strategic partners bottom-line answers, feedback, or results without them having to ask you (this shows you're on top of things). • Don't use flowery language, analogies, or metaphors in your communications (keep things simple). • Position clients and strategic partners as the one in charge (you're just the person on their team helping to make things happen).
The Market's Story: how to use the Ruler archetype to tell the story of today's market and illustrate your unique value	Keep things super simple when telling the story of today's market and illustrating your unique value using the Ruler archetype. In bullet points, show clients the bottom line: the headaches they'll have to endure, the time they'll waste, and the money they'll lose by not working with you in today's wild market. • Show the wildness of the market using stats or pictures. • Illustrate specifically how this wildness can destabilize their world. • Demonstrate how you can help them tame the chaos to get their bottom-line results.

TOPIC	COACHING TIPS

Your Sales Process: how to use the Ruler archetype to save time, be more productive, and improve your sales results	Imagine that you're the ruler of your domain, the CEO of your own company.
	
	• What are some performance-based goals for your business?
	
	  • I want to achieve X financial result by X date.
	
	• What are some things that threaten the stability of your business and may prevent you from achieving that result?
	
	  • Changing market conditions, increased competition, lack of consistent systems, etc.
	
	• What are one or two steps you can take now to tame the chaos, stabilize/anchor your business, and achieve your results?
	
	  • I can't control the market, but here's what I can do right now to take back control of this specific aspect of my business.

Your Strategy: how to "tame the chaos" and trigger profitable shifts in your business strategy	**Imagine yourself as the king or queen of your life and business. Ask yourself these questions:**
	
	• What are the items of chaos that are causing me and/or my team frustration right now?
	
	• How can I put boundaries on each item of chaos so I can begin taming each item in order of priority?
	
	• As for how to tame it:
	
	  • What's the root cause of each item of chaos?
	
	  • Is it possible and worthwhile to eliminate the root cause?
	
	  • If not, how can I limit the impact of that item of chaos with boundaries?
	
	Book Recommendations:
	
	• *The Power of Habit*
	
	• *The Challenger Sale*
	
	• *SPIN Selling*

Visit TheStorySeller.com and see *The StorySeller* podcast Episode 9 for more details.

CHAPTER 16

The Comedian Archetype

What's your favorite game?

No, not *that* one, silly! I'm talking about your favorite game when you were a kid. When I was a kid, I *loved* playing Monopoly. The only problem is that I took the game way too seriously. I would win often, which was great until it wasn't. I realized at one point that the game wasn't fun anymore for my siblings or others who were playing with me.

Maybe they weren't as competitive, or maybe I was too competitive. Who knows?

All I know is that at some point, the game stopped being fun. As I got older and started advancing in my career, I've found that the same principle applies in business. If I don't make the game fun for my coworkers, partners, or clients, they'll eventually lose interest, do a poor job, or just not be the team players I want them to be.

So every now and again (not too often because I much prefer being super serious and boring), I try to ask myself: how can I make this experience more fun and engaging for the other people playing the game of life and business with me?

That's how I've used the Comedian archetype in my business recently. How are you using it?

Characteristics of the Comedian Archetype

- Values living in the moment while enjoying life

- Wants to create joy for others and bring light to dark situations

- Skilled at using games, jokes, and humor to change perspectives

- Fears boredom and tries not to be boring

- Tends to be frivolous or irresponsible at times

Alternative Names for the Comedian Archetype

- Entertainer, Jester

Sample Comedian Brands in Popular Culture

- Las Vegas and gaming brands

Sample Comedian Archetypes in Popular Stories, Movies, and TV Shows

- Josh Lyman, *The West Wing*

- Pippin and Merry, *The Lord of the Rings*

TOPIC	COACHING TIPS

Your Story: how to use the Comedian archetype to build your personal brand	A Comedian brand is focused on giving its clients and strategic partners joy and happiness through a slightly edgy and anything-but-average experience.
	
	Here are a few tips you can use if you're trying to build a personal brand based on the Comedian archetype:
	
	• When working with clients and strategic referral partners, focus on how you provide a modern, fun, cutting-edge experience versus your competitors, who may be "same-old" average and boring. Examples:
	  • When STK Steakhouse first came into Atlanta, they took out billboards with the slogan "Not your daddy's steakhouse."
	  • When Quicken Loans/Rocket Mortgage first launched their digital mortgage product, they used a Super Bowl ad with the slogan "Push button. Get mortgage."

Your Client's Story: how to use the Comedian archetype to overcome objections	A Comedian client is looking for something to really grab their attention. They're not sold on you...yet. They're flighty and noncommittal, and it seems as if they're trying to test you or play games. So play the game with them, but on your terms! StorySelling Steps: • **Step 1:** Recognize and enjoy the Comedian archetype. That's the mode or mental state that the client is in right now. • **Step 2:** Illustrate how competing options or doing nothing would be "boring" or cause them to miss out. • **Step 3:** Illustrate how your products and services can help them stay on the cutting edge and be dazzling in their own right. StorySelling Tips to Overcome Objections with Clients or Strategic Partners Who Fit the Comedian Archetype: • "Seems like you want to experience X without paying the price of admission. Am I missing something?" • "Sure, I'm familiar with [the competitor the client is thinking of working with]. They're a great company. My grandmother used them when she bought her first house. Here's how we're different."
The Market's Story: how to use the Comedian archetype to tell the story of today's market and illustrate your unique value	Here are two tips you can use if you're trying to tell the story of today's market and illustrate your unique value using the Comedian archetype: • Have you ever played the slot machines in Las Vegas? Today's market is kind of like that—you never know what result you're gonna get when you pull the lever. Here's what you can expect when you work with me. • Today's market is like playing a game where the rules keep changing. Here's how we can help you keep up with all the changes so you can win the game.

TOPIC	COACHING TIPS
Your Sales Process: how to use the Comedian archetype to save time, be more productive, and improve your sales results	Here's a tip you can use to save time and improve your sales process with the Comedian archetype: • Try to "gamify" your business by rewarding yourself, your team, your clients, or your strategic partners when you hit certain targets or milestones. For example, make a deal with your spouse/partner where he or she gives you an extra __ if you completely stop work every day by X, but you have to give your spouse/partner an extra __ every time you don't.
Your Strategy: how to get on your Comedian platform and trigger profitable shifts in your business strategy	**Imagine yourself as a Comedian or an entertainer. Ask yourself these questions:** • How can I make sure I'm not the boring one of my industry? • How can I help my clients not be the boring ones of their industry? • How can I create fun and exciting experiences for my clients, strategic partners, or employees? • Is there a hobby I enjoy that I may be able to use to connect on a more human level with clients, strategic partners, or employees? **Book Recommendations:** • *Peak: How Great Companies Get Their Mojo from Maslow* • *Drive: The Surprising Truth About What Motivates Us* •*Hooked: How to Build Habit-Forming Products*

Visit TheStorySeller.com and see *The StorySeller* podcast Episode 10 for more details.

CHAPTER 17

The Friendly Neighbor Archetype

Have you ever been unable to do the things you want because you simply have too much on your plate?

I TEND TO COMMIT TO TOO MANY PROJECTS AT ONCE. MAYBE it's because I underestimate the amount of effort it will take to get things done. Maybe it's because I want to make the people in my life happy. Either way, I discovered that I just can't do it all! So I've tried to make a conscious effort to say no more often to projects or relationships that may detract from my core mission.

I've found that saying no to projects and relationships outside my core area of expertise has freed up my time and energy to be more effective at the projects and relationships inside my core area of expertise.

In essence, *I'm trying to be a better friend and neighbor to my core clients and relationships instead of trying to be everything to everybody.* I've found that taking this approach has helped me to achieve better results.

This is another way of implementing the 80/20 rule: Focus on the 20 percent of projects or relationships that make 80 percent of the impact on your life and business. Conversely, say no more often to the 80 percent of projects and relationships that have only a 20 percent impact on your life and business.

That's how I've used the Friendly Neighbor archetype in my business recently. How are you using it?

Characteristics of the Friendly Neighbor Archetype

- Values connection and relationships

- Doesn't want to feel alone and fears rejection

- Wants to feel safe and help others feel safe

- Wants to be a part of something special and enjoys being with people

- Finds meaning and joy in caring for others

- Tends to give too much of themselves and not know when to say no

Alternative Names for the Friendly Neighbor Archetype

- Caregiver, Lover, Loyal Friend

Sample Friendly Neighbor Brands in Popular Culture

- Community-oriented brands

- Chick-fil-A, State Farm

Sample Friendly Neighbor Archetypes in Popular Stories, Movies, and TV Shows

- Sam, *The Lord of the Rings*

- Jaime Lannister and Samwell Tarley, *Game of Thrones*

- Belle, *Beauty and the Beast*

TOPIC	COACHING TIPS
Your Story: how to use the Friendly Neighbor archetype to build your personal brand	The Friendly Neighbor brand is focused on serving the local community and protecting it from harm and outsiders.
	Here are a few tips you can use if you're trying to build a personal brand based on the Friendly Neighbor archetype:
	• When working with clients and strategic referral partners, focus on how you are local, community based, and relationship oriented.
	• Use folksy, family-oriented analogies and illustrations in your marketing.
	• Illustrate how you create value for the local community and how you lend a helping hand.
Your Client's Story: how to use the Friendly Neighbor archetype to overcome objections	The Friendly Neighbor client or strategic partner wants to feel safe and that they're part of something special. They want to make a difference in their family or community, and they are relationship oriented.
	StorySelling Steps:
	• **Step 1:** Recognize and connect with the Friendly Neighbor archetype. That's the mode or mental state that the client is in right now.
	• **Step 2:** Illustrate how the community has special needs that others may not understand. Show them how doing nothing or working with an "outsider" would cause them harm or danger.
	• **Step 3:** Illustrate how your products and services can help them stay safe and protected.
	StorySelling Tips to Overcome Objections with Clients or Strategic Partners Who Fit the Friendly Neighbor Archetype:
	• Use lots of testimonials and pictures of families in the local community who have benefited from working with you.
	• Illustrate how you are focused on a long-term relationship instead of a one-time transaction.
	• Illustrate the cost of working with someone who is not local or is unfamiliar with the needs of the community.
The Market's Story: how to use the Friendly Neighbor archetype to tell the story of today's market and illustrate your unique value	Here are a few tips you can use if you're trying to tell the story of today's market and illustrate your unique value using the Friendly Neighbor archetype:
	• "Navigating today's market on your own carries a lot of risk to you and your family because...[outline the top challenges facing them if they don't work with you]."
	• "My concern is that [the competitor option] doesn't account for what's happening here on a local level. Here's how that impacts you."
	• "Have you thought about the impact of working with someone who's not locally based like me? Here's the challenge of working with someone who's not familiar with the local market."

TOPIC	COACHING TIPS
Your Sales Process: how to use the Friendly Neighbor archetype to save time, be more productive, and improve your sales results	Here are two tips you can use to save time and improve your sales process with the Friendly Neighbor archetype: • Think of ways to get involved with your local community and how to highlight that involvement in your brand marketing and sales conversations. • Do special things as a team with your coworkers so they feel like they're a part of something bigger than themselves (lunches, happy hour, team outings, etc.).
Your Strategy: how to refocus on your community of Friendly Neighbors and trigger profitable shifts in your business strategy	**Imagine yourself as a Friendly Neighbor in the special community to which your clients or strategic partners belong. Then ask yourself these questions:** • What are the inside and outside forces causing harm or threatening harm to the community? • What would the impact be if I ignored that force and let it harm or threaten the community? • How can I reallocate my own attention and resources to my core community and help them avoid that bad outcome? **Book Recommendations:** • *This Is Marketing* • *Lovemarks: The Future Beyond Brands* • *Relationship Economics*

Visit TheStorySeller.com and see *The StorySeller* podcast Episode 11 for more details.

CHAPTER 18

The Artist Archetype

Have you ever tried to do something that you thought would just take a few minutes, only to find out painfully that you're in way over your head and that the project may derail your otherwise perfectly planned-out day?

THERE WAS A CONVERSATION I REMEMBER HAVING WITH MY then-six-year-old daughter about something that should have taken about two minutes. I quickly realized based on her questions that this was going to be more like a one- to two-hour conversation. I needed to have the conversation, but I just wasn't prepared to have it right then. So I asked my daughter if it would be okay if we spent some time the next day talking about it. She agreed, and we spent the next afternoon having a much-needed conversation about something that smarter-than-they-should-be six-year-olds talk about with their daddies around Christmastime.

In business oftentimes, I've experienced something similar where I get involved in a project or conversation that I initially anticipate might only take a few minutes of my time that day, but it turns out to be a much larger project than I could have imagined. My options?

- Option 1: Derail my day and do the thing right now.

- Option 2: Acknowledge I got in over my head and schedule the project for another time.

I've found that a lot of frustration can be avoided if I choose Option 2. I'm surprised that I don't choose Option 2 more often.

I've found that I need to do a better job of channeling my inner Artist to create my ideal day, removing from it any distractions that would tarnish its magnificence. I realize it will never be perfect, but I owe it to myself, my clients, or my family to at least try. I won't experience the ideal day every day, but experiencing it sometimes is better than never experiencing it at all.

That's how I've used the Artist archetype in my business recently. How are you using it?

Characteristics of the Artist Archetype

- Values excellence and takes pleasure in creating magnificent work

- Seeks to create something of enduring value

- Likes to express artistic skill and individualism

- Fears mediocrity or poor execution

- Tends to be overly dramatic or too much of a perfectionist

Alternative Names for the Artist Archetype

- Creator, Builder, Composer, Virtuoso, Maestro

Sample Artist Brands in Popular Culture

- Brands focused on empowering creators

- Canva, Adobe

Sample Artist Archetypes in Popular Stories, Movies, and TV Shows

- Don Draper and Peggy Olson, *Mad Men*

- Walter White, *Breaking Bad*

- Hermione Granger, *Harry Potter*

TOPIC	COACHING TIPS
Your Story: how to use the Artist archetype to build your personal brand	An Artist brand is focused on helping its clients and partners create something of enduring value. Here are three tips you can use if you're trying to build a personal brand based on the Artist archetype: • When working with clients and strategic referral partners, focus on how you make their life easier so they can "do what they do best." • Position yourself as a partner who can help them create something magnificent. • You'll most often find this archetype with potential strategic partners who want to do something in-house instead of outsourcing it. Position your brand as something that can be privately labeled or used to create an all-inclusive, holistic experience or to fill any potential gaps in their business.
Your Client's Story: how to use the Artist archetype to overcome objections	The Artist client or strategic partner fears that if they partner with you instead of doing it themselves, it will result in an inferior result or poor execution. Their objections will typically revolve around this fear and their desire to maintain control over the process or outcome. StorySelling Steps: • **Step 1:** Recognize and appreciate the Artist archetype. That's the mode or mental state that the client is in right now. • **Step 2:** Illustrate the various distractions and hurdles they face in creating their magnificent work. This demonstrates a clear grasp of their challenges. • **Step 3:** Illustrate how your products and services can help them overcome those challenges and bring their vision to life. StorySelling Tips to Overcome Objections with Clients or Strategic Partners Who Fit the Artist Archetype: • "Option 1 is to do it yourself. And that's totally okay. Here's what that looks like... Option 2 is to work with me, and here's what that looks like..." • "What's the primary concern holding you back from partnering on this with someone like me?" • "Could you paint a picture for me of what a successful process or outcome would look like for you?"
The Market's Story: how to use the Artist archetype to tell the story of today's market and illustrate your unique value	Here are two tips you can use if you're trying to tell the story of today's market and illustrate your unique value using the Artist archetype: • Illustrate ways that the market today is more complicated than they realize and how those added complications can cost them time and money if they go it alone ("Here's why it's not that simple... Have you thought about how you're going to handle that?"). • Show them a picture of the market volatility or how a deal can fall through due to unforeseen circumstances. Then illustrate how partnering with you can avoid that unpleasant outcome.

TOPIC	COACHING TIPS
Your Sales Process: how to use the Artist archetype to save time, be more productive, and improve your sales results	• Reference Something Artistic about You: What is something unique about you personally that you can inject into your business to give it some authentic, artistic flair? Are you a great cook? Are you a musician or an artist? Do you have an interesting hobby? Can you perhaps discuss or show some of your creations or hobbies in your conversations or social media posts to give your marketing a more authentic look and feel? • Discover Something Artistic about Your Client or Strategic Partner: Do you have a way of capturing personal information about your clients and then sending them articles or gifts that would be meaningful to them based on what you discovered? What about taking notes in your CRM about personal things you notice about clients/strategic partners during the course of normal conversation (such as their hobbies, favorite sports team, or alma mater)?
Your Strategy: how to channel your inner Artist and trigger profitable shifts in your business strategy	**Imagine yourself as a Master Artist, seeking to create significant, lasting value. Then ask yourself these questions:** • What specific value do I seek to create by my work, and for whom? • What's the long-term impact of that value? • What distractions are standing in my way or preventing me from doing what I was born to do? • How can I eliminate those distractions and simplify my day-to-day life so I can focus my time and attention on work that matters? **Book Recommendations:** • *The Big Leap* • *The War of Art* • *The Hero and the Outlaw*

Visit TheStorySeller.com and see *The StorySeller* podcast Episode 12 for more details.

CHAPTER 19

The Scholar Archetype

Have you ever dealt with a customer service rep who was super annoying or otherwise just plain stupid?

I'VE FOUND THAT THE STUPID ONES DON'T SEEM TO KNOW anything while the annoying ones are way too over-the-top in the way they share their knowledge. I've always had a fear of being like the super-annoying person who's over-the-top in what they share.

Recently, I've tried to conquer this fear by sharing what I believe to be useful insights in story format. Everyone likes a good story! I know I certainly do. What if we could channel our inner Scholar and use the expert knowledge we've acquired over many years of study and hard work, and become more effective storytellers?

That's part of the main reason I created this book and coaching series: for you, and for me. I'm learning just as much as you as we take this journey together. Here's an idea I'd like to run by you:

What if you could create a weekly coaching video or social media post where you just tell a story—something you learned, observed, or discovered that week that could be useful to your target audience?

I think you'd really enjoy it!

Characteristics of the Scholar Archetype

- Values truth, knowledge, and wisdom

- Seeks to learn and teach at every opportunity

- Skeptical, curious, and inquisitive in pursuit of mastery

- Respects intelligence and fears being ignorant or duped

- Tends to overanalyze and be indecisive

Alternative Names for the Scholar Archetype

- Sage, Philosopher, Teacher, Prophet

242 • THE STORYSELLER ADVENTURES

Sample Scholar Brands in Popular Culture

- Brands focused on excellence or expertise

- Harvard University and other Ivy League schools

Sample Scholar Archetypes in Popular Stories, Movies, and TV Shows

- Tyrion Lannister, *Game of Thrones*

- Alex P. Keaton, *Family Ties*

- Yoda and Obi-Wan Kenobi, Star Wars

TOPIC	COACHING TIPS
Your Story: how to use the Scholar archetype to build your personal brand	The Scholar brand is focused on helping its clients or strategic partners achieve excellence or expertise. Here are three tips you can use if you're trying to build a personal brand based on the Scholar archetype: • Give your clients and strategic partners unique tips, insights, and insider information that's not readily available through your competitors. • When working with clients and strategic referral partners, focus on how you educate them so they can achieve better results. • You could create a branch or division of your business to educate strategic partners and give them a cutting edge, something like "Homebuyer University" for consumers or "Top Producer Mastermind" for strategic partners.
Your Client's Story: how to use the Scholar archetype to overcome objections	The Scholar client or strategic partner respects expertise and values knowledge and wisdom. They want to make an informed decision, and they sometimes tend to overanalyze. StorySelling Steps: • **Step 1:** Recognize and think with the Scholar archetype. That's the mode or mental state that the client is in right now. • **Step 2:** Illustrate the various challenges of finding or deciphering the info they need to make a smart decision. • **Step 3:** Illustrate how your products and services can help them cut through the "noise" and make an informed decision. StorySelling Tips to Overcome Objections with Clients or Strategic Partners Who Fit the Scholar Archetype: • Use stats, charts, and graphs to illustrate your recommendations, and be prepared to share the source of your information so they know it's reliable. • Use testimonials (particularly with strategic partners) from people in similar situations who have benefited from working with you. • For the person who is overanalyzing, ask questions like these: • What would need to be true in order to move forward one way or another? • What exactly is holding you back? • Is there something specific you're looking for in these details to help you make an informed decision?

TOPIC	COACHING TIPS
The Market's Story: how to use the Scholar archetype to tell the story of today's market and illustrate your unique value	Here are two tips you can use if you're trying to tell the story of today's market and illustrate your unique value using the Scholar archetype: • Use stats, charts, and graphs to illustrate the volatility or danger of the market, along with why clients and strategic partners need access to your "inside information" or "expert guidance." • Create videos and educational materials on what's happening in your local market or in your niche in the market so you build a brand as the #1 expert in your market.
Your Sales Process: how to use the Scholar archetype to save time, be more productive, and improve your sales results	Here are two tips you can use to save time and improve your sales process with the Scholar archetype: • Identify a niche of target strategic partners (such as real estate agents or financial advisors who specialize in a certain niche). Set aside time each day to read up on their industry and become conversationally fluent on their challenges. For example, if you're trying to get more referrals from real estate agents, read publications like Inman. If you're trying to get more referrals from financial advisors, read publications like Financial Planning magazine. • Focus on educational opportunities that keep you in front of your target niche on a regular basis. For example, join their associations, conduct continuing education workshops for them, and organize local mastermind groups.
Your Strategy: how to put on your Scholar robe and trigger profitable shifts in your business strategy	**Imagine yourself as a wise Scholar. Ask yourself these questions:** • How can I become such an expert in my industry that people would pay to hear my sales pitch because they'd learn so much? • What kind of problems does my target audience have, and how can I help solve those problems with my knowledge and expertise? • How can I share my knowledge and expertise in a way that would make me happy and give me joy while creating massive value for my target audience? **Book Recommendations:** • *The Voice of the Master* • *The Hero with a Thousand Faces*

Visit TheStorySeller.com and see *The StorySeller* podcast Episode 13 for more details.

CHAPTER 20

The Rebel Archetype

Have you ever felt so angry that you were compelled to do something radical or revolutionary in response?

OUR SOCIETY IS MORE FRAGMENTED AND ANGRIER NOW THAN at any point that I can remember in my forty-two years on the earth. I, like you, have seen things in the past few years that have completely eroded my confidence in certain people and institutions that were once very sacred to me. I, like you, have gotten very angry when I've seen these things, and I've often wondered how best to respond. In those times, I look to my personal history and the "rebels" who've come before me for guidance.

My family is originally from Lebanon. Although I was born and raised in the United States, my mom is from Lebanon and my dad is third-generation Lebanese American. My mom's dad (my grandfather) was somewhat of a revolutionary in his day. He belonged to a political party that stood against the status quo of corruption that has dominated Lebanon for the past century.

Despite his righteous anger and rebellious tendencies, my grandfather was also a pragmatic, loving, generous man. It was his love for his family and his pragmatism as the leader of his family that informed the decision to emigrate to the United States in the 1970s when his country was gripped by strife and being torn apart by civil war.

It was his pragmatism and love that informed his actions, not his anger. He found a way to channel his anger into a better future for his family. There are dozens of his descendants now who either wouldn't exist or would have an otherwise miserable existence had it not been for his decision to leave his homeland and come to America. For that, I'm very grateful.

My gratitude for his pragmatism is one of the conduits that allows me to channel my own anger and perform my own version of rebellion against the injustice I see in my society. I've found that the most radical response I can have to my anger is to feel grateful instead. That transformation of negative energy into positive energy allows me to be productive and present for the people in my life who matter most to me.

In essence, my rebellion is against the Rebels and Adults of my generation who feel their sacrifice is somehow greater than that of the generations who came before them. My form of revolution is to create value despite the unnecessary obstacles that others create for me along my Journey. My form of revenge is to live a well-lived life as best I can in sickness and in health, during good times and during bad times, with gratitude for the many people, past and present, who make it possible.

Along those lines, allow me to express my gratitude to you and to acknowledge the sacrifices you make every day to make life better for your family and clients despite the obstacles you encounter along your Journey. Thank you for being you and for doing the things you do!

Characteristics of the Rebel Archetype

- Values complete independence and seeks to overthrow the status quo

- Focused on revolution, disruption, and/or revenge against "the establishment" or, as I like to call them, the Adults

- Gets frustrated with boundaries, any form of authority, or feeling powerless

- Thrives in chaos and is attracted to shock-and-awe tactics

- Fears being minimized, being insignificant, or making only incremental progress

- Looks for ways to highlight role as a misfit or an outsider

Alternative Names for the Rebel Archetype

- Outlaw, Misfit, Outsider

Sample Rebel Brands in Popular Culture

- Brands focused on rebellion against the status quo

- Harley-Davidson, early-days Apple, Fox News Channel, Black Lives Matter Movement(s), LGBTQIA+ Movement(s)

Sample Rebel Archetypes in Popular Stories, Movies, and TV Shows

- Batman

- Young Michael Corleone, *The Godfather*

- Dolores Abernathy, *Westworld*

- Pablo Escobar, *Narcos*

TOPIC	COACHING TIPS
Your Story: how to use the Rebel archetype to build your personal brand	The Rebel brand is focused on empowering its clients or strategic partners to be different, gain independence, or otherwise achieve victory against the Adults who are holding them down. Here are three tips you can use if you're trying to build a personal brand based on the Rebel archetype: • When working with clients and strategic referral partners, focus on how you're completely different from what they may be used to from your industry. • Use surprising, unexpected, and edgy illustrations or marketing headlines. • Position yourself as a misfit who is uniquely positioned to work with misfits. This is especially useful if your target ideal client is part of an underserved segment of the market that is typically ignored by the Adults of your industry.
Your Client's Story: how to use the Rebel archetype to overcome objections	A Rebel client is someone who feels left out or otherwise ignored by the Adults of your industry. If they are beaten down, you can rally them to victory. If they are angry, you can help them channel their anger in positive ways to get the results they want. StorySelling Steps: • **Step 1:** Recognize and identify with the Rebel archetype. That's the mode or mental state that the client is in right now. • **Step 2:** Illustrate how the "adults" or "establishment" of your industry has kept them in chains or prevented them from being the best version of themselves. You can even blame the chains on "fake news," a "confusing market," or "lack of options" for "people like us." • **Step 3:** Illustrate how your products and services help the client break their chains and free themselves. StorySelling Tips to Overcome Objections with Clients or Strategic Partners Who Fit the Rebel Archetype: • Clearly illustrate how the Adults of your industry (your competitors) have ignored this segment of the market and how now is the time for a change. • Clearly illustrate how, by working with you, your client or strategic partner can get what's rightfully theirs—before it's too late.
The Market's Story: how to use the Rebel archetype to tell the story of today's market and illustrate your unique value	Use shock-and-awe illustrations, headlines, and stories when talking about the market. • Show how the market is leaving them behind if they don't act now. • Illustrate how the Adults have figured out how to play the market—and win. • Explain how your mission is to help underserved "people like us" navigate the market and get the successful outcome we deserve.

TOPIC	COACHING TIPS
Your Sales Process: how to use the Rebel archetype to save time, be more productive, and improve your sales results	Imagine that you're the leader of a revolution, and your mission is to overthrow the status quo of your own day-to-day business in favor of a better version of it. What's the most radical thing you can do to "shock" your business into a new direction? For example: • What have you been completely afraid to do for months or years? • What's the worst-case scenario that could happen if you do that thing you're afraid to do? • What's the best-case scenario that could happen if you take the plunge and do the thing you're afraid to do? • Just do it! Take the plunge. We only live once. Let's make it count!
Your Strategy: how to set aside your chains of Disappointment and Unrealistic Expectations and trigger shifts in your business strategy	**Imagine yourself on the Battlefield of Rebels.** • Option 1 is to eventually die on the Battlefield as a meaningless failure after living as a meaningless loser. • Option 2 is to set aside your chains of Disappointment and Unrealistic Expectations and live the productive life you were born to live. Victoriously. Reinvented. In one of the other realms. I know that's harsh. But that's reality. Whose reality? Mine. And now, yours. I hope you choose Option 2! After you've made that smart choice, consider taking these three steps (they changed my life!): **1. Leave behind the old version of your life or business.** • Make peace with your past and completely let it go. This includes people, relationships, and opportunities you've lost, along with expectations that were unfulfilled. Mourn those losses, but don't dwell on them. • If your pain and losses are as deep as mine, which they probably are, you will very likely benefit from the advice and care of qualified mental health professionals. I have done so, and I highly recommend it. Unfortunately, pain, depression, and anxiety are common companions along the StorySeller journey. An entire book should be written about it. In fact, I'm writing two books about it. The next two books in this series will deal with those challenges. I'll share with you some best practices I've learned that I think will be very useful to you. **2. Define your new/unique skills or resources.** • What are the lessons you've learned or the "magic powers" you've acquired on your Journey? **3. Use your experiences to create a fresh start and new beginning.** • Use the archetypes to create a compelling personal brand with your personal story and unique skills. You can join TheStorySeller community for support, resources, and daily inspiration. You don't have to be alone on this journey!

TOPIC	COACHING TIPS
	Book Recommendations: • *The Prophet* • *The Hero with a Thousand Faces* • All the books I recommend in Additional Resources, specifically those in the category of Spiritual Journey, Inspiration, and Allegory

Visit TheStorySeller.com and see *The StorySeller* podcast Episode 14 for more details.

Conclusion

To My Fellow StorySellers,

I hope you enjoyed my story! I've found that by understanding the nine human archetypes explored in this book, I can wear different "hats" and be the person I need to be in the moment. I can channel my inner Magician, or my inner Warrior, or my inner Ruler, etc. I can ask myself "ridiculous questions" and come up with creative solutions to difficult problems in life and business. I've shared my findings and methods with you in this book because I truly believe they can be as life-changing for you as they've been for me!

I believe StorySellers are great adventurers, traveling through the Realms of Reality selling the people they encounter in each Realm the best version of themselves. Over the years and in my travels, I've had the privilege and honor of meeting many such great StorySellers.

As of the time of this writing, I've trained and coached over ten thousand of America's top sales and business professionals, mostly in the housing and financial industry. I've learned that my primary archetype is that of Scholar, and the clients I serve are primarily Warriors.

I've learned that the best formula for success, for me, is to give my clients what they want (tools to achieve victory) in a way that allows me to get what I want (focus my time and energy on learning and teaching). That's when I'm happiest, most fulfilled, and most productive as my "best self."

The biggest mistakes I've made in business have been when I've strayed too far outside of that simple formula. When I fail, it's mostly when I get involved in business ventures that are outside my primary archetype or when I fail to communicate with my clients in a way that resonates with their primary archetype.

Of course, nobody is always one thing, and we're all Rebels at heart. Even so, understanding the archetypes and story structure has certainly helped me to better navigate the ever-changing Realms of my Reality. That's why my best advice to you is this:

1. Discover your primary archetype so you can stay true to it and be comfortable as yourself.

2. Discover your ideal client's primary archetype so you can better speak their language and win their business.

3. Bridge the gap between the two archetypes and find your Unique, Authentic Winning Story (UAWS).

To that end, I've made it my life's work to help you on your Journey as you navigate the ever-changing Realms of your Reality. I would consider it an honor if you'd find value in working with me!

This book has a "plain language" sister podcast called *The Story-Seller*. Episodes 6–14 of *The StorySeller* podcast go deeper on each of the nine archetypes. You can listen for free wherever you listen to podcasts or on our website at TheStorySeller.com.

As an added bonus, I've created a free coaching program called *The StorySeller 30-Day Business Growth Journey*. The *30-Day Journey* gives you a step-by-step system to implement the concepts in this book, delivered to your email inbox each day. It will help you avoid burnout, find more meaning in your work, and grow your business. You can enroll for free at TheStory-Seller.com.

In addition to *The StorySeller* book, podcast, and *30-Day Journey*, our website contains other tools and resources to help you create and live your Unique, Authentic Winning Story (UAWS). We provide many resources for free to individuals and small business owners, and we have paid programs for larger teams, organizations, and enterprises. You can participate in our programs as is, or we can integrate and embed them into your existing training and coaching programs. We can also customize our programs for your organization via private workshops and keynote speeches.

This book and step-by-step guide is only a sampling of what you'll get if you decide to work with us on a more formal basis.

If you're interested, please visit TheStorySeller.com.

Acknowledgments

MY LOVE OF LYRICAL PROSE AND WORDPLAY TRACES BACK TO the Lebanese folk music and poetry from my childhood, which still inspires me to this day. I'm sure if you look closely enough, you'll find loosely paraphrased lyrics from those influences scattered throughout my writings. You'll most definitely find loosely paraphrased thoughts and words influenced by the Lebanese poet and thinker Gibran Khalil Gibran.

My way of understanding my own story through allegory also traces back to my childhood. As I was growing up, my mom would use metaphors and analogies to decipher for me and my siblings the lessons and stories our dad told us. He was (and remains) a great storyteller, but he is, admittedly, often cryptic in the way he communicates. I suppose I'm the same way at times, which I'm sure is a challenge for my own wife and children! In this sense, my parents were and remain the original StorySellers in my life. For that and for you, I am eternally grateful. Your lessons of love and gratitude will never be forgotten. In fact, they'll be memorialized for as long as humans can read, in this book and in all my writings.

I'm grateful to each one of my five younger siblings, who've influenced me in the most surprising ways. I very much cherish the memories of our childhood and the friendships we built together in our youth, and by working together in our family businesses. May God illuminate your Journey through Life as brilliantly as you've illuminated mine. We were (and remain) Children of Life together. You first taught me the meaning of friendship. May our love and friendship remain forever young.

I'm grateful to my grandparents, whose love and many sacrifices made it possible for me to live my story. I strive each day to honor your memory with my work and to make you proud by my words and actions. I hope that my Life's work and Life's story are a positive reflection on your legacy of love, our family heritage, and our family name.

I'm grateful to my father-in-law, whose wisdom and kindness encouraged me in my darkest moments and helped me through some of my most important crossroads. I often imagine myself sitting down with you, drinking coffee, as you advise and guide me through some of my most important life and business decisions. I will forever cherish your memory and the valuable lessons you taught me.

To my wife, Mandy: You introduced me to the Playground of Lovers, and may Life always be our Playground. You taught my heart how to sing again when you opened your heart to me. You are my inspiration now and always. Every celebration of Life in this book is a celebration of you and the Life we've created together. None of it would exist without you. May the music and laughter of our loving home inspire our beautiful children to never stop dancing.

To my children, Valentina, Marcos, and Marcelo: I've written this book for you and the generations who come after you! My sincerest desire is to give you the best roadmap I can to help you discover and live your Story as you journey through Blue Oceans of Life and Business.

May you always see the Door of Choice and choose the Road of Love. May you explore the Realms of Reality with grace and Magic, and find within them many hidden Treasures. May this book series, along with my entire body of work, give you a head start in life and business, and help you overcome the challenges that come your way. You are Warriors and Rebels, Rulers and Comedians, Explorers and Magicians, Scholars and Artists. The world is your Friendly Neighborhood, so don't ever believe yourself to be an Outsider. May your Life's work and your Life's story be your love letter to humanity and your offering to our God.

To you, the Reader: The same goes for you! May my words and stories bring to life the beautiful music of your own Story and encourage you to discover and live your UAWS.

To my friends, clients, colleagues, and coworkers, and all the men, women, and persons of the US mortgage, financial, and real estate industry who have supported me and my work throughout the years: Your influence on me and my work is too great to list. I am truly grateful for each and every one of you!

To Danny: You still inspire me in more ways than you'll ever know. I can't wait to dance the dabke with you in heaven, in front of God and everybody.

Forever yours and with undying gratitude,

Gibran Nicholas
Alpharetta, Georgia
October 1, 2022

Additional Resources

I DIDN'T INVENT ARCHETYPES OR THE USE OF STORY structure in business. I've simply shared with you what I've learned over the years through my own experiences—so far. I'm not done learning!

In fact, I've compiled below a list of books that have most influenced my thinking. This list is not exhaustive, and I'm not done being influenced! I consider these books to be my primary influences, along with my own experiences.

If you look closely enough, you'll find in my writings loosely paraphrased thoughts and ideas from all the following books and writers. Some of these influences appear prominently in this story, and others may appear more prominently in the next two books of this series. Perhaps you'll enjoy the books on this list and find them to be as useful on your journey as I've found them to be on mine.

Some of the following authors (the ones who are alive at least!) may offer training courses, consulting services, or coaching programs to go with their books. Please invest in yourself and make use of their resources as a follow-up to this book or as a complement to my system. Enjoy!

Story Structure and Archetypes
in Life and Business

- *The Hero with a Thousand Faces* and *The Power of Myth* by Joseph Campbell

- *The Hero and the Outlaw* by Margaret Mark and Carol Pearson

- *StorySelling for Financial Advisors and Your Client's Story* by Mitch Anthony

- *Fascinate* and *How the World Sees You* by Sally Hogshead

- *Building a StoryBrand* by Donald Miller

- The works and speeches of Tony Robbins

- *Relationship Breakthrough* by Cloe Madanes and Anthony Robbins

- *The Five Love Languages* by Gary Chapman

Marketing, Sales, Strategy, and Business Philosophy

- The comprehensive works and writings of Seth Godin, most notably for me his daily blog, and his books *Tribes* and *This Is Marketing*

- *Blue Ocean Strategy* by W. Chan Kim and Renee Mauborgne

- *Never Split the Difference* by Chris Voss

- *Start with No* by Jim Camp

- *The Art of War* by Sun Tzu

- *The War of Art* by Steven Pressfield

- *Playing to Win* by Roger L. Martin and A. G. Lafley

- *Lovemarks: The Future beyond Brands* by Kevin Roberts

- *How I Raised Myself from Failure to Success in Selling* by Frank Bettger

- *My Life in Advertising* and *Scientific Advertising* by Claude Hopkins

- The comprehensive works and writings of Nassim Nicholas Taleb, most notably for me *The Black Swan,*

Fooled by Randomness, Antifragile, and *The Bed of Procrustes*

- *The Power of Habit* by Charles Duhigg

- *Drive: The Surprising Truth about What Motivates Us* by Daniel Pink

- *Relationship Economics* by David Nour

- *SPIN Selling* by Neil Rackham

- *The Challenger Sale* by Matthew Dixon and Brent Adamson

- *The Big Leap* by Gay Hendricks

- *Shoe Dog* by Phil Knight

- *The Signal and the Noise* by Nate Silver

- *The Ultimate Sales Machine* by Chet Holmes

- *Mojo: How to Get It, Keep It, and Get It Back if You Lose It* by Marshall Goldsmith and Mark Reiter

- *Peak: How Great Companies Get Their Mojo from Maslow* by Chip Conley

- *Hooked: How to Build Habit-Forming Products* by Nir Eyal and Ryan Hoover

- *Zero to One* by Peter Thiel

- *Tribal Leadership* by Dave Logan, John King, and Halee Fischer-Wright

- *Compete to Create* by Dr. Michael Gervais and Pete Carroll

- *The Coaching Habit* by Michael Bungay Stanier

- *The Tipping Point* and *Blink* by Malcolm Gladwell

- *Finite and Infinite Games* by James Carse

- *The Infinite Game* by Simon Sinek

- The works and writings of Zig Ziglar, most notably for me *Born to Win*

Novels and Allegorical Stories

- *The Alchemist* by Paulo Coelho

- The writings and stories of Og Mandino, most notably for me *The Greatest Salesman in the World*

- The writings and stories of Gabriel Garcia Marquez, most notably for me *One Hundred Years of Solitude*

- The writings and stories of Ayn Rand, most notably for me *The Fountainhead* and *Atlas Shrugged*

- The Greek myths

- *The Arabian Nights*

- The many books and writings of Dr. Seuss, Mark Twain, Charles Dickens, Victor Hugo, Alexandre Dumas, and countless others

- Many movies and TV shows, including the classics and modern epics

Other Writings, Speeches, and Poems

- The comprehensive work, writings, and speeches of Winston Churchill, Martin Luther King Jr., Maya Angelou, and a few of America's founders and past presidents, including Teddy Roosevelt's "The Man in the Arena" speech

- *If* by Rudyard Kipling

- *Little Gidding* by T. S. Eliot

- *Desiderata* by Max Ehrmann

- *The Road Less Traveled* by Robert Frost

Spiritual Journey, Inspiration, and Allegory

- The Bible

- The Bhagavad Gita

- The Upanishads

- The Dhammapada

- *Becoming Nobody* by Ram Dass

- *The Power of Now* by Eckhart Tolle

- *The Miracle of Right Thought* by Orison Swett Marden

- *Man's Search for Meaning* by Viktor Frankl

- The comprehensive work and writings of C. S. Lewis, most notably for me *The Problem of Pain, The Weight of Glory, The Four Loves*, and *Till We Have Faces, a Myth Retold*

- *The Divine Comedy* by Dante Alighieri

- *Pilgrim's Progress* and *The Holy War* by John Bunyan

- *Paradise Lost* by John Milton

- The writings of St. Augustine, St. Thomas Aquinas, and countless other saints

- *The Holiness of God* and *The Consequences of Ideas* by R. C. Sproul

- *Desiring God* by John Piper

- *The Sacred Romance* and *Wild at Heart* by John Eldredge

- *Meditations* by Marcus Aurelius

- The writings of the Persian poet Rumi, specifically *The Essential Rumi*, as translated by Coleman Barks

- The comprehensive work and writings of the Lebanese poet and thinker Gibran Khalil Gibran, most notably for me *Broken Wings*, *The Madman*, *The Voice of the Master*, and, of course, *The Prophet*

About the Author

Gibran Nicholas is the author of *The StorySeller Adventures* and the founder and CEO of Momentifi, a sales training and content marketing platform that provides daily coaching and expert marketing content to thousands of housing and financial professionals. Over ten thousand entrepreneurs, business leaders, and sales professionals have graduated from Gibran's training and coaching programs. Many of them have implemented his StorySelling system and have become top producers.

Gibran became a millionaire by age twenty-five and lost everything two years later, only to regain it all, plus invaluable life lessons, over the next decade. He shares with you many of those lessons in this book, and in his weekly podcast. Gibran's primary focus is to help you and your team use archetypes and Story-Selling to find more meaning in your work and grow your business. You can find weekly episodes of *The StorySeller* podcast and daily coaching tips at TheStorySeller.com.

Gibran lives in Alpharetta, Georgia, with his wife, Mandy, and their three children. Gibran is a lifelong student of business, politics, religion, and the human experience. Connect with Gibran, his team, and your fellow StorySellers at TheStorySeller.com.

Call to Action

What's your archetype?

Visit TheStorySeller.com to get your FREE assessment!

Looking for a keynote speaker for your group or event?

Visit TheStorySeller.com to book Gibran as a speaker.

Want to get daily coaching tips for how to use archetypes and StorySelling to stay motivated and grow your business?

Visit TheStorySeller.com!

CPSIA information can be obtained
at www.ICGtesting.com
Printed in the USA
BVHW082309040123
655594BV00001B/1